"THE BROKEN PASTOR"

THE BROKEN PASTOR

The Voice of a Pastor for the Ear of the Church

STUART D. REYNOLDS

Ambassador International
GREENVILLE, SOUTH CAROLINA & BELFAST, NORTHERN IRELAND

www.ambassador-international.com

The Broken Pastor

The Voice of a Pastor for the Ear of the Church

ISBN: 978-1-935507-35-2

Design & Printed by Bethel Solutions

Ambassador International
Emerald House
427 Wade Hampton Blvd
Greenville, SC 29609, USA

Ambassador Books and Media
The Mount
2 Woodstock Link
Belfast, BT6 8DD, Northern Ireland, UK

www.ambassador-international.com

The colophon is a trademark of Ambassador

Email - reynolds.stuart1@sky.com

This book is dedicated to every battered and broken pastor and their families, beginning with my own wife, Helen; daughters, Heather and Leah; and mother, Helen, who oftentimes, from afar, has no less suffered with us.

"Those who sow in tears will reap with songs of joy.
He who goes out weeping, carrying the seed to sow,
will return with songs of joy,
carrying sheaves with him."

Psalm 126:5-6

Contents

Introduction

Who Is *'The Broken Pastor'*?

"The Broken Pastor" is a real person, and, sadly, not in the minority when it comes to the reality scars and scrapes of pastoral ministry. Like most pastors, I am BATTERED and BRUISED, and I seek to write humbly out of this pain with simple honesty, in the prayer-filled hope that, by the mercy and grace of God, some will find enlightenment, liberation, and even a measure of healing in the process.

To be struggling and *"broken"* is not the badge of shame many unhelpfully considerate it to be, but may well be the testimony of tried-for-faithfulness and the knowledge of fighting in God's fight – which is very far removed from the typical *"civil wars"* and *"petty squabbles"* of many local churches! So many pastors are hurting, seeming to be constantly on the verge of quitting, feeling like failures, having the last embers of self-worth kicked and stamped out of them, also contending with the added burdens of guilt in themselves and censure from their denominations if they were to ever admit to and express these things.

This particular *"Broken Pastor"* has been preaching for thirty years, and, at the time of writing, has been in full-time Pastoral Ministry for nearly twenty. Who I am really is of no consequence. The exact locations of where I have had the privilege of pastoring are not required knowledge…but that I am a real pastor – a *"Broken Pastor"* – is all the reader needs to know. For no matter the identity of pastor, location, or church, for the pastor, in particular, who reads, it is himself he is reading about, where he is, how he is – *"BROKEN"*!

However, this book is not only for pastors – *"broken"* or otherwise. Again, it is the prayer-filled hope and working intention of the writer that also reading these words will be Church Board members along with the wider congregation. This is a book for the whole church! For the ones reading who are not pastors, these are truths, confessions, burdens you need to hear and know about, not only for the benefit of your pastor, but also for the wellbeing of the Church as a whole, and ultimately self: *"For we must all appear before the judgement seat of Christ, that each one may receive what is due him for the things done while in the body, whether good or bad"* [2 Corinthians 5:10].

Everything you will read has actually happened and has been recorded as accurately as is possible. For obvious reasons, names have either been left out or changed. I am grateful for the freedom that has enabled me to write with uninhibited frankness, even bluntness. The stories, again, are real. The feelings and the pain are raw. And, just maybe, just maybe, it will help one other pastor who reads it, to find a companion in brokenness, and, perhaps, help to rediscover the merits of their Calling, being given a helping hand to go on, because *"Broken Pastor"* – IT WILL BE WORTH IT TO HOLD ON!

One final word – this is a *"work in progress"*! I have neither resigned nor retired from ministry. I still know brokenness, the insensitivity of some of those we serve, the hostility of the true enemy of our souls, and the deep doubts we have about self. My battle, like yours, is still being fought. My story is not over yet. My *"conclusion"* is still to be written. I am still in the trenches, still in the struggle, still living with my brokenness…and yet living and breathing and proving…still!

You need to know that everything, and most of everyone, I write about is still alive. I need to protect both the innocent and the guilty, both victim and offender. I have no desire to bring dishonour on the Church…but I do want to write with liberty and power…that you can FEEL and KNOW…and be RELEASED in SAFETY to say – *"The 'Broken Pastor' is me!"*

CHAPTER 1
IN THE BEGINNING...

"The word of the LORD came to me, saying:
'Before I formed you in the womb I chose you, before you were born I set you
apart....'" [Jeremiah 1:4-5]

As pastors, if we didn't believe that we would never have entered pastoral ministry – that ministry is God's idea, along with our place in it. Pastor, do you remember how it was when you took your first steps – in both preparation and actual practice – into ministry? We had great dreams of what we would achieve...lofty expectations of how it would be, like the early Christ-ones we read of in Acts 17:6, we too were going to *"turn the world upside down"* for Jesus Christ! We envisaged Church Board members who would always be understanding, *"Church-folk"* who would always be appreciative, the un-saved who would flock to hear us, having undisturbed study time to prepare sermons and Bible studies which would almost fall *"pre-packaged"* from Heaven itself, and a home life that would be protected, where the needs of the pastoral family are sensitively recognized and faithfully respected by the Church, thus allowing the *"manse"* (*"parsonage"*) to be a well-balanced place of refuge, where it would always be remembered that it is the pastor who is paid and not his wife, and that the pastor's children should be treated like all the others, because they are no different from all the others.

"Wonderful!"

A little boy said to his father, *"Dad, let's play darts. I'll throw, and you say, 'Wonderful!'"* The fact is, in those early stages of ministry, those *"beginning"* days when much of the above was coming together and being processed, there was no shortage of such encouragement for us. The Church – no matter the denomination or affiliation – is always in need of pastors, and what a boost it is for all to hear of young people testifying to a call to service, giving themselves to it, in the locating, testing, and developing of their ministry gifts and graces. *"Wonderful!"* was neither long in coming or short in supply when it did come.

Ironically – surprisingly – for me, at any rate, the first persons to shake my confidence, dampening my high ideals and expectations, dimming the light on my bright *"visions",* were other pastors who had been in the ministry hot-seat for some years, and their *"voice of experience"* painted a different picture, sounding a more down-beat note, as they too rehearsed the former days when they had said what I did, setting out with big dreams, high hopes, having great confidence in the help that the Church who recognized and confirmed their calling, would always be there to offer them, with their continuing support and encouragement – *"Wonderful!"* These pastors were neither fallen or failing, they were not trying to be destructive. In their own way, they were seeking to protect the likes of me. You see, all of them were weary, and many of them were broken.

"Friendly Fire!"
Not a day goes by when we do not hear of further fatal casualties among our troops in the war zones of the world to which we are committed. Such a high price but worthy of the goal – freedom from oppression in the establish-ing of democracy. It is hard enough to accept the fatalities which result from contact with the enemy – that is to be expected – but when the casualties are the result of what has come to be called *"Friendly Fire,"* the point of it all gets lost in the wastefulness and folly of it all because it was not necessary. It's the same in the Church – and especially with pastors – which makes it worse on both counts. The Bible tells us that the Church is the *"Body"* of Christ and that pastors are amongst the *"gifts"* Christ has given to His Church [see 1 Corinthians 12-13 & Ephesians 4] . It is one thing to be bruised and broken by the enemy…but when it is your "own"?

It was Charles Swindoll who made the candid observation of how the

Church has this shocking tendency to shoot its own wounded! That's why we have, not only "Broken Pastors" – but pastors who are trapped in their brokenness, not being able to be healed, and the result is that they ultimately give up in the job, or pack in by walking away from the job…with the result that many pastors' children grow up with a chip on their shoulder regarding the Church, and more crucially, a grudge against God! How sad, how very, very sad – not only should it not be, but it really doesn't need to be. As pastors, many of us will submit ourselves to some kind of training – either full-time at Bible College, or spells of intensive study, or even just being mentored by an older pastor, if the facility for more recognized training is not there. My point is that, we train pastors to look after the people in the Church – and that is absolutely right – but when are Churches ever trained in how they should look after their pastors?

I now pastor an independent Church, but I grew up in and began pastoring in a denomination – a heritage and preparation I will always be grateful for, they nurtured and trained me well. Although it was never said outrightly, there was always a reluctance in me to really come out and speak of my struggles and troubles and doubts and fears, because there was this lingering suspicion that it would be *"noted"* and *"filed,"* someday being *"used against you in evidence"* – quite frankly, hindering some future prospect of "advancement" within the Church. I remember one time after preaching being taken aside by an older pastor and being told, *"Never preach about your weaknesses! Never! You are the pastor and the congregation must not know that you struggle!"* Many pastors can relate to that expectation. And so, not wanting to be a disappointment to the people we serve and certainly not wanting to dishonour God, we suffer and struggle in silence, trapped in our *"brokenness."*

For many, this is how we are, how it is…but it was not so…*"In The Beginning…!"*

Marked By God!
Pastor do you remember when that was, when you first became aware that God did have a plan for your life? He not only touched your heart in your

salvation – giving you a place of belonging in His Church – but He also stirred your heart in service to Him – also giving you a place of usefulness in His Church. What an amazing thought – that the God Who made the universe, hanging the stars in space, creating worlds and setting their orbits, establishing the borders of the land and the limits of the sea, that this God also saw you and knew you, *"before you were born"*, *"choosing"* you, setting out a place for you, establishing a time for you, creating a space for you.

A census taker knocked on the door of a little cottage in the middle of nowhere. A fellow came to the door. The census taker said, *"The Prime Minister has sent us across the country to find out how many people live in the United Kingdom."* The man replied, *"I'm sorry you came all the way out here to ask me because I don't have the faintest idea!"* Pastor, when God marked you for service He did not make a mistake – He knew what He was doing, what He was asking. And you did not misunderstand Him, for you had come to know His voice and could not ignore the pleadings of the Holy Spirit stirring your heart. You were and are marked by God!

Motivated For Service!

There is a school of thought that says, *"Fight your call! Resist it as much as you can! If you can do anything else do it!"* I call it, doing the *"Jonah-thing"*! And there are those who are like that, and even need the process of that, whereby their motivation for service takes them in the wrong direction, and there are examples in God's Book of that – Jonah and Moses for starters! I was the other way, I was always keen to get into service for God. My trouble was not resistance but patience. I could never wait to get to my *"Nineveh!"* Not only was there not anything else I could do – and be fulfilled and at peace with God in – but there was also nothing else I wanted to do. That God would even glance in my direction, never mind stop and call me, has always amazed me, and, at the same time I'm sure, infuriated satan, because hell just can't comprehend what God sees in us and why He would ever choose to use us when He has so many other means at His disposal. What a great motivation for service. The song says, *"I want to give my life for something that will last forever, O I delight, I delight to do Your will!"* [Mark Altrogge, c. People Of Destiny/

Copycare Ltd 1982]. To be allied with the Holy Spirit in the work of Christ at the pleasure of the Father.

"Meant For This?"

Although, *"In The Beginning"* I ran to ministry and not away from it, it's as the years have passed that I have increasingly entertained doing the *"Jonah-thing"* – that's what brokenness does to you, where you don't so much want to run away, but crawl away! As I listen to myself I hear myself sounding like the old pastors of my younger days. I've said to my wife more than once that I feel as if I'm becoming the *"Victor Meldrew"* of the pastorate – something I have never wanted…but again, that's what brokenness can do to a pastor! [Victor Meldrew is an ageing grumpy man in the B.B.C. sitcom, *"One Foot In The Grave"*]

As noble and right *"giving our lives for something that will last forever"* and *"delighting to do God's will"* are, we nevertheless, live in a world that is so ordered to be set against us achieving that. We are to minister in a still fallen world, to people who are not Saved, and to Saved people who are still not perfect, including ourselves! How many of us have done our best, given our utmost, seeking to be faithful, and have found ourselves, like John the Baptist, in an unbelievable place of *"confinement"*, and with John the Baptist begin wonder and ask Jesus: *"Are You the One Who was to come, or should we expect someone else?"* [Matthew 11:3] *"Jesus, I'm not sure anymore!…I never thought it would be like this?…Is this what it's all about?…Am I meant for this?"* Some pastors wonder if they got their calling wrong, they question if they have displeased God, they ask if they took a wrong turn, they doubt they are in the right place anymore… *"Meant for this? I would never have believed it!…Meant for this?"*

The HEALING Starts Here Because The HEARING Starts Here!

There are some reading this and perhaps it has made you feel worse than you were before you picked it up! Sometimes the process of healing involves more pain. Others may think this has been a futile exercise in unhealthy self-absorption, nothing more than a "pity-party"! In Job 2:8 we find Job "*taking a piece of broken pottery and scraping himself with it as he sat among the ashes.*" There is a place for that, a time for that, a need for that. Pastors need to find a way of acknowledging their bruises and brokenness, and of tending to them. That's what these words have been about – speaking out for and on behalf of pastors that they may begin to be heard and thus begin to be healed. Pastor, it's not wrong to be surrounded by "*ashes*" – the "*ashes*" of a wounded heart and wasted dreams. Pastor, it's not sinful to stop and sit down and acknowledge that and begin tending to your "*sores*" [see Job 2:7] and what makes you "*sore*" – Job's "*sores*" were the scars of what it cost him to be faithful to God, as are your's. In John 11, Jesus, Who had already declared His being "*the Resurrection and the Life*" and Who knew what He was going to do, nevertheless, lingered over Lazarus' grave – "*weeping*" – just in the same way as Job sat among the "*ashes*" and gave vent, expression to his "*sores*" It was at this point that HEARING began to lead to HEALING…as Job's friends, and ultimately God, came around him. That's what we need – friends and God to come around us, amidst the "*ashes*" of our brokenness.

Pastor, your HEARING is the beginning of your HEALING! You need to know, YOU are NOT ALONE! You are NOT the ONLY "Broken Pastor". This "Broken Pastor" hears you and speaks (writes) for you because he has heard and is also speaking for himself. When you stand in those crisis places in life, being there for those under your care…when you have to faithfully visit those "difficult" people…when you stand to preach before a congregation of faces which do not look friendly and even look bored…please know that this "*Broken Pastor*" prays for you…and wants to shout to you for your encouragement – "*Wonderful! Wonderful! Wonderful!*"

"*See all the wounded,*
Hear all their desperate cries for help,
Pleading for shelter and for peace.
Our comrades are suffering;
Come, let us meet them at their need -
Don't let a wounded soldier die.

Obeying their orders
They fought on the front lines for our King,
Capturing the enemy's stronghold.
Weakened from battle,
satan crept in to steal their lives –
Don't let a wounded soldier die."

["Wounded Soldier" by Dony McGuire & Reba Rambo, c. 1983, Kingdom Music]

It is precisely and uniquely here that the community of the Church needs to step in with the loving sensitivity of practical support, which is, no less, a supernatural effort, enabled by the Holy Spirit through all those who will. As the chorus of the song above expresses it:

Come, let us pour the oil,
Come, let us bind the hurt;
Let's cover them with the blanket of His love.
Come, let us break the bread;
Come, let us give them rest;
Let's minister healing to them –
Don't let another wounded soldier die."

My prayer is that *"The Broken Pastor"* will become, for those of us who will, a beginning place, even like the place of our call, *"In The Beginning!"*

Yours in *"the fellowship of His sufferings,"*
The Broken Pastor!

CHAPTER 2

BE PATIENT

" A discerning man keeps wisdom in view, but a fool's eyes wander to the ends of the earth." [Proverbs 17:24]

These thoughts and shared experiences are mainly for those considering full-time service in the ministry for God, especially younger people. Those of us who are now older and in ministry will do well to recall these times in our own lives, and those who have never received such a *"call"*, need to understand what it is like and what it means for those who have, and often why they are like they are because of what they are having to work through.

The Ship Of Hope, Called *"Dreams!"*

What a keen observation Proverbs 17:24 is, not just on ministry, but for and in life – how much we miss of the present, by focussing too much on where we might be one day, by dwelling on where we – in our opinion - should be now, but are not, and the result is we miss the possibilities of today and overlook the need for today in where we are…how foolish! Many talk of waiting for their *"ship to come in"* – that, in itself, is a lesson in patience, but what many fail to realize, often until it is too late, is that our *"ship"* will never come in if we never send it out in the first place. The *"ships"* which do, eventually, come in tomorrow, will only ever be the ones we send out today – from wherever we are.

"Patience" For Ministry!

I was 15 years old and on a Christian Youth Holiday in Portugal. It was around this time when my first stirrings of a call to ministry were clarified and

I began to testify and share with others to that end. On that Youth Holiday I met and quickly got close to an older German Pastor – probably one of my first real mentors, outside of my own father – and he passed on to me a real gem of counsel. Over and over again, he would quietly say to me in his distinctive German accent, *"Be patient! Be patient!"* Before other helpful advice would come flooding in – like seeking to identify God-given gifts and graces for ministry, and being directed and encouraged to *"Read! Read! Read!"* – this was the first piece of counsel I was given, *"Be patient!"* And now, some thirty years later, I not only remember it, but still struggle with the mastery of it. To take up the words the Apostle Paul used in regard to another matter – *"Not that I have already obtained all this…."* [Philippians 3:12] It however remains true and right – the *"answer"* we need for today and the *"key"* that will lead us into our dreamed-of, hoped-for, and worked-for tomorrow.

As I mentioned in the opening chapter, for me, a recognized call to minister for God was something, especially in those earlier, younger days, I had always run towards and actively, even breathlessly pursued. I must have been so difficult to be around, because I was constantly on the look out for opportunities to minister. I even saw the necessary training a Bible College affords, as a hurdle to be overcome, an intervention, and not as a vital help that would only come into its own, years later, over the long haul (more of that in Chapter 3).

I often recall as a young person growing up in Church and those words of Jesus from Revelation 22:12 – *"Behold, I am coming soon!"* All the older folk would be saying, *"Amen. Come, Lord Jesus."* And there was me, this young person, eager for ministry, and my heart would be whispering, *"Amen, Come Lord Jesus…but not too soon!!!"* I was saying that not because I wanted to get out into the world and *"sow my wild oats"*, it was because I wanted the chance to serve Jesus and be a pastor and preach His Word! I almost begrudged four years of a Theology Degree – *"What if Jesus comes back before I finish and get a real chance to put all this 'training' into practice?…What if there are no openings for ministry, no vacant pulpits and pastorates by the time I get out?"* You see, I looked upon the needful place of *"today"* like a prison sentence!

So much for me heeding my mentor's valuable advice, *"Be patient!"* There was still so much immaturity in me, even arrogance, too much of *"self"* – and God in His wisdom and goodness would not overlook it, thus encouraging it to take a deep, and ultimately destructive, root.

However, what do we do and where do we go with a stirring call to service, and a like-passion to serve? It needs to be expressed – if it is suppressed it will die – and a lot of the above experiences, were the out-workings of all this, giving vent to it in trying to go with it. Just like a young child's first steps and words are often *"trial by error"* so is the coming to terms with and working out of a call from God, especially at the beginning, and especially with a young person. Just consider Joseph – seventeen years old - who already had his dreams, but without patience, to the severe annoyance of his brothers, to say the least (see Genesis 37).

I am thankful to God for the people he placed around me who would let me neither take impulsive short-cuts, nor impatiently sell myself short– starting with my father, who would not let me go to Bible College straight from school, but insisted I work in the *"real world"* for at least two years, and ending, in those formative years, with a firm Bible College Principal who just quietly refused to let me leave Bible College early when an opportunity for a pastorate presented itself, which I was keen to fill. Both these men, at those two points – going to Bible College too quickly and then leaving to soon - just told me what I was going to do, and that was that! We all need people in our lives like that, to whom we have to listen because of who they are, as they patiently protect us from our impatient selves!

I know the feelings, frustrations, and fears of the young and thrilled would-be pastor, preacher, missionary, who may be reading these words – and you just love Jesus and want to serve God and *"go"* for Him now. Your *"Call"* is neither a mistake on your part nor a cruel joke on God's. There is a very important Bible verse you would do well keep close by you, because you will need it and, if you will be patient, prove it. It is found in Isaiah 66:9 – " *'Do I bring to the moment of birth and not give delivery?' says the LORD....*"

What God has conceived in you, He will bring to birth. But that takes time – patience – because of what it means and brings. Consequently, it is not only tomorrow that matters, but also today! The Most High God, Who in His fleshly incarnation spent nine months as a foetus growing inside a human womb, knows all about patience.

"Patience" In Ministry!

Marriage has wittily been described as being like *"...a city under siege – the people outside are desperate to get in, while those inside are desperate to get out!"* Many pastors have come to feel that way in their *"marriage"* to the ministry. As we've already noted, while many younger, prospective pastors are keenly asking, *"When can I start?"* there are many older, already-pastors who are wearily pleading, *"When will it end?"* That *"ship"* they sent out in their younger, brighter days seems to have been *"lost at sea"*! Like my earlier experiences with Bible College, so it is with ministry as a whole – not only can you jump in too quickly – but you can also bail out too soon! I have often wondered how many marriages would have been saved if the couple involved had stuck at it a while longer? How many great Churches – not necessarily *"big"* – have never been because both pastor and people called a halt with each other too soon? How many have left the ministry before their time, absenting themselves from the end of the *"pier"* where, for so long, they had faithfully stood, waiting for that ship of hope, called *"Dreams"*?

I don't ask these questions rashly, thoughtlessly, insensitively, or unknowingly. There have been many times I have wanted to jump off the *"pier"* never mind just slip away from it in defeat! When such happens, it is not a time for adding to the desperate feelings of guilt, condemnation – there is no cause for that, but rather for sadness, even mourning over what has been lost, and may never now be.

Perhaps there are pastors reading these words, who, like me, are still seeking to be faithful in ministry, but are frankly, up to now, secretly disappointed. What have we given our lives for? What has been achieved? We have still never got to where we thought we should be, thus never knowing what we thought could be. As I write these words I have been pastoring for twenty years, yet I frequently have this feeling of starting-over, still beginning. Sometimes it feels like a game of *"Ministry Monopoly"* – constantly passing *"GO!"* but never getting to collect our equivalent £200 that will help build and lead to better things. How many of us have given up hoping and dreaming and searching and looking and moving any longer because we just can't take the let-down any more, there has been one too many false dawns? The result is, that in giving up on tomorrow, we too, miss out on the meaning and even the miracle of today, returning to the same place as our would-be successors.

For us who need *"Patience"* In Ministry, the second part of Isaiah 66:9 is for us – *"... 'Do I close up the womb when I bring to delivery?' says your God."* Why would God close the door on us, giving up and sinking the *"ship"* He built and first placed in our hearts? God is extravagant but He is not wasteful and He is not a liar. What if our *"time"*, our *"fruitful"* place, our *"ship"*, our highest point was just for one moment where the impact we would make, would be one that God chooses to make through only us and not another, even just for one day – but the ripples and result of which would last forever? Would that be worth holding on for? Would such merit our *"Patience"* In Ministry?

In his book, *"Why Revival Tarries"*, Leonard Ravenhill wrote, *"Brethren, in the light of the 'bema seat,' we had better live six months with a volcanic heart, denouncing sin in places high and low and turning the nation from the power of satan unto God rather than die loaded with ecclesiastical honours and theological degrees and be the laughing stock of hell and of spiritual nonentities."* ["Why Revival Tarries", p.104. Bethany House Publishers, c.1959].

What if, for us, this is still yet to come? Our finest hour was still yet to be? We must be *"Patient"* In Ministry – no matter how long, how hard, how bad. It will be worth it because He is always worthy of it.

Noah's *"Parking Place"*!
A cartoon quips, *"DON'T GIVE UP. IT TOOK NOAH SIX MONTHS TO FIND A PARKING PLACE!!!"* Would-be pastor – God has a place and a

time for you, and He knows where and when: *"Be Patient!"* Already-pastor – God remembers your place, and He has a time for you that will yet prove to be your finest hour: *"Be Patient!"*

Isaiah was given to speak about *"The Servant Of The LORD"* we all are. *"…Before I was born the LORD called me; from my birth He has made mention of my name. He made my mouth like a sharpened sword, in the shadow of His hand He hid me; He made me into a polished arrow and concealed me in His quiver* [waiting for the right time and the best place]. *He said to me, 'You are My servant…in whom I will display My splendour.' But I said, 'I have laboured to no purpose; I have spent my strength in vain and for nothing. Yet what is due me is in the LORD'S hand, and my reward is with my God.'"* [Isaiah 49:1c-4].

> *"He didn't bring us this far, to leave us;*
> *He didn't teach us to swim, to let us drown;*
> *He didn't build a home in us, to move away;*
> *He didn't lift us up, to let us down.*
> *No, He didn't lift us up, to let us down."*

[by Phil Johnson, c.1978 BMG Music]

Pastor – old, new, yet to be – *"Be Patient"* your finest hour will surely come!

Yours in *"the fellowship of His sufferings,"*
The Broken Pastor!

CHAPTER 3
BIBLE COLLEGE

"Do your best to present yourself to God as one approved, a workman who does not need to be ashamed and who correctly handles the word of truth."
[2 Timothy 2:15]

On its own, Bible College will never do what Paul encourages and instructs young Pastor Timothy over in 2 Timothy 2:15...but Bible College certainly helps and has an important and necessary place in the process of it as a preparation for ministry, in the clarifying of our call, identifying our gifts, addressing fundamental weaknesses, stretching and testing our entire selves by giving us the tools whereby we can pursue a lifetime of personal growth into ministry, in the careful and conscious working-out of our full potential as servants of the Most High God. The whole atmosphere of a college campus also helps to equip us socially in the different kinds of people ministry will inevitably surround us with. In the unique environment a college provides, these social factors are also points of pressure and challenge because we are living so closely and even intensely with each other, and we have to get on together and work together. However, that resolve will and needs to be tested, beginning with the social flaws in self. A pastor is given the unique placing in peoples' lives where he will be given to see them at their very best and worst! Though often unpleasant and even painful at the time, it is, nevertheless, good for us that we be exposed to the contrasts and contradictions of people and their up-close personalities and performances, beginning to learn by experience how to cope with them, before we are let loose on a congregation, with the dangerous consequence that we may want to help kill them to put us out of our misery and not help cure them to put them out of their misery!

One of the reasons why I wanted to go straight to Bible College from leaving school was because I thought it would be wonderful, oh, so wonderful, to be able to study the Bible everyday, and to live alongside other Christians who were doing the same things. It was not long before my high ideals were grounded in the lower-life-realm called *"REALITY"!* As the old verse puts it:

"To live above with saints we love
Will certainly be glory!
To live below with saints we know –
Well, that's another story!"
{source unknown}

I believe the experience of Bible College can give us a hunger for excellence in every facet of service because we are given the ability through learning and its consequences to know the difference between what is the mark of the *"approved workman…doing his best"* and that of the well-intended but sloppy *"amateur"*, who does not really know what he is doing, because he has never fully given himself to it – pastoral ministry is not a Sunday-hobby, it is the calling of a lifetime because it demands our whole selves committed to *"doing our best"!*

The Parable Of The First-Aider!

It would be impossible to calculate how many lives have been saved by first-aid training. Imagine the scene: a busy high street, suddenly a man collapses, the bustling crowd around him stops and stares, suddenly some-one emerges, gets down on the ground beside the man and quietly speaks to him, asking his name to see if he is conscious. She then makes sure the man's airways are unblocked and puts him in the recovery position. He stops breathing, and she starts administering *"cpr"* until the paramedics arrive to take over. Her prompt and enlightened actions have saved this man's life! That's great and should be recognized and applauded, and used to encourage others to get first-aid training. However, it would be absolute folly to give this heroine a white coat, put a stethoscope around her neck, and start calling her *"Doctor"!* If she exhibits potential in the practice of medicine she would be set on a course of study and given formal training. Why should pastors, who are given to *"practice"* on the for-ever part of humanity – the soul - be any different?

Where would the Church be without what is commonly called its *"Lay Ministers"?* It is one thing to preach on occasion – like it is to save a life on the street – but it is quite another and demands something essentially different to minister over the long haul, to preach Sunday by Sunday, year after year, to the same congregation, living with them, bearing with them in the circle of life.

"Martin, Thou Art Lazy!"

Jesus says, *"...do not worry beforehand about what to say. Just say whatever is given you at the time, for it is not you speaking, but the Holy Spirit"* [Mark 13:11]. How many have used this not only as an argument against the formal preparation of Bible College, but also against faithful preparation in the hard work of the study, not realizing that the context of what Jesus says is not preaching but persecution? Mark 13:11 begins with *"Whenever you are arrested and brought to trial...."* If these *"enlightened radicals"* – as they like to see themselves – had only spent some time at Bible College, they would know that we must always set and consider a text within its context, otherwise you proceed on an unsupportable pretext, which leads to, not *"enlightened radicals"* in the pulpit but *"embarrassing rascals"*!

It is said that one Sunday morning as Martin Luther ascended the stairs of the pulpit to preach he prayed, *"God, Thou knowest how busy I have been this last week, and my study for preaching has suffered, please give me a word for today!"* To which the Holy Spirit whispered to his heart, *"Martin, Thou art lazy!"*

The disciplines I live by today were impressed on me in the four years I spent training at Bible College. As in much of life, I did not appreciate the value of what I was doing and what was happening in me at the time, it is only after the fact, as the years of ministry have rolled on that I have ever-more realized how well I was taught and prepared. The Bible College I rashly and immaturely considered to be a hurdle that had to be endured and jumped was indeed a vital help that will never be surpassed and exhausted.

The Greatest Bible College Myth?

God calls His servants, to whatever realm it may be. God calls, a Bible College can clarify the call, and the Church must ultimately confirm the call, but it is God Who calls. A Bible College cannot make a preacher any more than it can make a pastor, or teacher, or missionary, but it can nurture and develop, by imparting the skills to rightly use the tools of ministry. Perhaps the greatest piece of knowledge I graduated from Bible College with was two-fold: the knowledge of how much I did not know, but also the taught-skill of being able to rightly use the tools that I might increase in knowledge and excellence. I will never graduate – either personally or pastorally – from being a student in the Word of God, but I have been equipped with the tools, the necessary means, of rightly studying and faithfully and effectively communicating Its truth, in concert with the anointing of the Holy Spirit. Is part of our *"doing our best to present ourselves to God as approved workmen, correctly handling the word of truth"* not our making every effort to surround ourselves with the best teachers and give ourselves to learning the disciplines and effecting the skills necessary to our work, understanding that none of this come apart from the anointing of the Holy Spirit? We don't want dry pastors and ministries but dynamic and durable ones.

Please Don't Just Teach The Truth – Tell Us The Truth!

This would be my plea to all Bible Colleges, and it has come as a result of a particularly painful experience I had with a ministerial student who had come on a pastoral placement to a local Church I pastored. From beginning to end, it was a nightmare – from basic social skills, to personal discipline, to the necessary gifts and graces for ministry – this poor fellow, was just a non-starter. At the end of his six-week placement I had to write an assessment. My biggest disappointment was with the Bible College in question. In my report I asked, *"How is it that a pastoral ministry student can be in his final year of a four year degree and these issues not have been identified and addressed?"* Both the student and the College had nowhere to turn. It was a tragedy, but sadly, not unique. Is this not part of the reason as to the high fall-out rate of pastors from the ministry – that some should never have been there in the first place? We all know how *"pushy"* Christian parents can be, and how a call testified to early on, and subsequently tested may not ultimately lead to full-time ministry. Like a bride on the eve of her wedding who knows the marriage is wrong, but goes ahead because of all the effort and preparations which have been made and she doesn't want to disappoint, so many have wrongly entered ministry because of this same pressure of expectation and the burden of not wanting to be a disappointment. With many Denominations there is also a real crisis in terms of new pastors, and the impulse is strong to take the short-term view of easing the immediate needs, without asking the right questions, and the problem is relieved only temporarily and, ultimately, even worsened because of discouragement all round, when it does not work out because it was never right and should therefore have never been. It is here that Bible Colleges really come in to their own, and need to stand up and tell the truth, and carefully deflate some *"bubbles"* in the relative safety of the College, not leaving it to the severity of the pastorate itself where the *"bubble"* can be fatally burst, leaving an individual feeling not only humiliated but betrayed, asking *"If you saw it coming – why didn't you tell me?"* The account of Dr. Billy Graham's Bible School Principal telling him he would never amount to anything in ministry is legendary, and should be remembered, but there are many more occasions, where I suspect, such straight talking was needful but tragically silent!

A Word Of Thanks To My Mentors!

Much of the learning a Bible College affords is not only academic but also relational. I have counted it a privilege to have rubbed shoulders with and been taught by some truly godly men and women. Back in Glasgow there's a little phrase: *"It's better felt than 'telt!"* My College Lecturers helped stir in me a thirst for learning, introducing me to a host of classic Christian writings and their writers, giving me a healthy respect and fundamental understanding of God's *"Book"* the Bible is. Some of them had gone through as pastors what I was yet to, and they knew, and the benefit of their insights and experiences, in the sharing of their pastoral-pains, remains invaluable. By their own personal dedication to their God-called work, they showed me how it never pays to sell our hearers short in shoddy, shallow workmanship. Their own spirituality in the integrity of their personal character was the biggest lesson of all. Why would I have ever wanted to miss out on that? Indeed, where would I be now had I done so? Certainly not writing this!

For this pastor, even in his brokenness, Bible College remains *"my place of tested dreams and little regret!"* I could not commend such a place to you more highly.

Yours in *"the fellowship of His sufferings,"*
The Broken Pastor!

CHAPTER 4

THE LOCAL CHURCH 'POPE'

"…but Diotrephes, who loves being in charge, denigrates my counsel. If I come to you, you can be sure I'll hold him to account for spreading vicious rumours about us. As if that weren't bad enough, he not only refuses hospitality for travelling Christians but tries to stop others from welcoming them. Worse yet, instead of inviting them in he throws them out."
["The Message" paraphrase of 3 John 9-10]

The *"Protestant"* Pope!

The Roman Catholic Church has one Pope at any given time – and he resides, for most, far away in Rome! There are more *"Protestant"* Popes, reigning much closer in many local Churches, and as is their wont – they *"protest"*! The *"Local Church 'Pope'"* may be just one person or may be represented in the dynasty of a formidable Church family who have been there *"forever"*, it seems, and through whom all things happen and without whom nothing happens. The *"Local Church 'Pope'"*, horrors of horrors, may even be a former pastor(s)! That is a tragedy if not also a travesty all on its own.

A pastor will not have to wait long before meeting the *"Local Church 'Pope'"* – such will, in their own way, make themselves known. The *"Local Church 'Pope'"* would rather have a pastor who can be controlled than have to fight, and so, usually, the pastor will be given time to settle in, discover their *"place"*, and, by consequence, come to know his. There may even be a few initial skirmishes over little items, small points, where a couple of warning *"shots"* are volleyed across the bows of the pastor, just to remind him of what is what and who it actually is he is dealing with. Ultimately, a place will be reached, a situation will arise over which the pastor will, subtly but clearly, be given an invitation/ultimatum – depending on the perspective – to either kiss the *"pope's"* ring in submission and join the *"payroll"* or incur the wrath of 'papal' excommunication from within the very Church he is pastoring. This *"Broken Pastor"* remembers sitting in a parishioner's home and being politely but firmly told, *"Pastor, you need to know* [and he mentioned the names of three prominent families in the Church] *are not pleased with you!"* That was all that was said, but that was enough, for the unspoken message/threat – again depending on your perspective – was *"Get your act together and fall in line with us…or else!"* If such is resisted, the battle-lines are drawn and *"support"* is withheld. From that moment on, everything the pastor says and does is analysed, he is ostracized and his pastorate sabotaged in a guerrilla campaign of discontentment and disruption. It is here that most pastors break because of how and where and from whom the *"attacks"* come.

When *"Beauties"* Become *"Beasts"*!

What is terribly sad about Diotrephes [3 John 9] and all other *"Local Church 'Popes'"* before and after, is that to have the place of influence and trust they have come to occupy in the local Church they must have done something right and good and praiseworthy. Many pastors have found to their unspeakable dismay that the very ones who started out as their closest advisers, most trusted confidants, greatest supporters and firm family friends become the *"Local Church 'Popes'"* who turn against them and can't get them out – *"excommunicated"* - quickly enough. *"Diotrephes"* would not have been able to do enough for the pastor when he first came – he would have helped with transport, given love gifts to the pastoral family, over long years given faithfully and sacrificially to the life of the local Church. When it comes to excellent Churchmanship *"Diotrophes"* is in a league of his own, and he is lauded and applauded as such – but then something happens. A pastor comes in, who does not *"know"* and thus *"bow"* like the others do, and the wrong sense of *"ownership"* that *"Diotrephes"* has come to have – often allowed him by other well-intentioned but weak-willed Church folk – is revealed, and that is when and why *"'Beauties' Become 'Beasts'"*.

Over the years, I have found this excerpt from Marshall Shelley's book, *"Well-Intentioned Dragons"* to be of great insight:

"Dragons, of course, are fictional beasts – monstrous reptiles with lion's claws, a serpent's tail, bat wings, and scaly skin. They exist only in the imagination.

But there are dragons of a different sort, decidedly real. In most cases, though not always, they do not intend to be sinister; in fact, they're usually quite friendly. But their charm belies their power to destroy.

Within the church, they are often sincere, well-meaning saints, but they leave ulcers, strained relationships, and hard feelings in their wake. They don't consider themselves difficult people. They don't sit up at nights thinking of ways to be nasty. Often they are pillars of the community – talented, strong personalities, deservingly respected – but for some reason, they undermine the ministry of the church. They are not naturally rebellious or pathological; they are loyal church members, convinced they're serving God, but they wind up doing more harm than good.

They can drive pastors crazy…or out of the church.

Some dragons are openly critical. They are the ones who accuse you of being (pick one) too spiritual, not spiritual enough, too dominant, too laid back, too narrow, too loose, too structured, too disorganized, or ulterior in your motives.

These criticism are painful because they are largely unanswerable.

How can you defend yourself and maintain a spirit of peace? How can you possibly prove the purity of your motives? Dragons make it hard to disagree without being disagreeable.

Relationships are both the professional and personal priority for pastors – getting along with people is an essential element of any ministry – and when relationships are vandalized by critical dragons, many pastors feel like failures. Politicians are satisfied with 51 percent of the constituency behind them; pastors, however, feel the pain when one vocal member becomes an opponent.

Sightings of these dragons are all too common. As one veteran pastor says, 'Anyone who's been in ministry more than an hour and a half knows the wrath of a dragon.' Or, as Harry Ironside put it, 'Wherever there's light, there's bugs.'"

{Used by permission "Well-Intentioned Dragons" by Marshall Shelley. Published by Bethany House, a division of Baker Publishing Group,, 1994, pp.11-12}

How many Church "Beauties" become Church "Beasts" in this way? It's not that the pastor is being insensitive and unappreciative – and that can happen – it's because "...*Diotrephes, who loves to be first...*" does not get his own way and is not given his *"place"*. That is why, for this *"Broken Pastor"*, it is unwise, because it is ultimately unhelpful and self-deating, to have Church furniture, rooms, even whole buildings, named after people. It is right that we acknowledge and honour those who work hard amongst us [see 1 Thessalonians 5:12-13] but when such become virtually *"untouchable"* because of who they are and all they have done, we have a *"sacred cow"* in our midst, the modern equivalent of the Israelites' snake on a pole [see Numbers 21:4-9 & 2 Kings 18:4].

Those who think they have a right to expect because of all they have earned should remember Jesus Christ of Whom the Apostle Paul wrote "...*made Himself of no reputation....*" [Philippians 2:7, K.J.V.] In the carnal *"reward-culture"* which the Church has become entangled in, all of us would do well to long, honestly, and deeply meditate on the parable Jesus told His disciples in Luke 17:7-10:

"Suppose one of you had a servant ploughing or looking after the sheep. Would he say to the servant when he comes in from the field, 'Come along now and sit down to eat?' Would he not rather say, 'Prepare my supper, get yourself ready and wait on me while I eat and drink; after that you may eat and drink'? Would he thank the servant because he did what he was told to do? So you also, when you have done everything you were told to do, should say, 'We are unworthy servants; we have only done our duty.'"

Breaking The Cycle And Slaying The Dragon!

How many *"Dragons"* – *"well-intentioned"* or otherwise – have been allowed to reign in terror, wreak havoc in the local church and wreck ministries because pastors abdicate and will not face them down, not to silence them, but to slay them?

A lot of what happens in Church-life is cyclical. This is especially so when it comes to *"popes"* and their pastors. Often you will find that the ordeal the present pastor is undergoing has been the lot of the pastor(s) before him. The dragon was ultimately pacified through getting his own way – the pastor *"out"* – with the same potential just waiting to happen again. Pastor, this is one battle you will have to face and fight to the end! The cycle of *"The Local Church 'Pope'"* needs to be broken, the dragon needs to be slayed – not just silenced until the next time, for the next pastoral-victim – but slain. Such is not only the best thing you can do for the ministry God would give you in the Church you serve, but is also the best thing that can happen for the dragon, that the *"Beauty"* in them will be restored to rise again. A pastor who is comfortable with confrontation – even relishing it - is probably in the wrong job, and needs to test his motives. I never like confrontation, but what gives me the courage of commitment is the knowledge of what my purpose is. I am committed to helping those under my pastoral care to get to Heaven with as little regret as possible. How grieved these *"Well-Intentioned Dragons"* will be when they face Jesus, because of what we allowed to continue, and by, even passive consequence, affirmed and thus deepened them in. I will have a part in answering for that. We are our *"brother's keeper"* [Genesis 4:9]. We need to be committed to slaying the *"Beast"* that the *"Beauty"* might be saved!

The *"popes"* of Jesus' day were many of the Pharisees. He had such patience with them – acknowledging their position, every Sabbath giving them their place – He is the Most High God, remember. But there came a day, a time, an issue over which Jesus could no longer give way – " ' *My house will be called a house of prayer for all nations.' But you have made it a den of thieves"* [Mark 11:17, N.I.V.]. Pastor Jim Cymbala refers to this as, *"The Day Jesus Got Mad!"* {"Fresh Wind, Fresh Fire," by Jim Cymbala, Zondervan Publishing House, c.1997, p.67}

Even the Apostle John had his day, his time, his issue – *"…but Diotrephes who loves to be first, will have nothing to do with us. So if I come, I will call attention to what he is doing, gossiping maliciously about us…."* [3 John 9-10, N.I.V.] We may have expected such tough-talk from the more abrasive Paul, or even the impulsive Peter, but John? The Apostle of love? The Apostle John had put up with enough and it was now time to square up to Diotrephes and take on that *"Dragon"* he had become.

There comes a day, a time, an issue for us all as pastors where we must not flinch or abdicate, but stand our ground, square up and turn up for the fight, breaking the cycle, slaying the dragon – *"No more! No further! Enough!"*

The Potential *"Pope"* In All Of Us!
For all the brokenness there is among pastors, there is, nevertheless, a strong *"personality-cult"* in the ministry today. We not only need to recognize this but also that we too, however small or limited our sphere of service, can fall victim to it. If we should not take on board and believe the worst of what our opponents say about us – and we shouldn't – then neither should we believe and take on board the best of what our most faithful supporters would say of us.

How wise these words from Dag Hammarskjold are:
"Around a man who has been pushed into the limelight, a legend begins to grow as it does around a dead man. But a dead man is in no danger of yielding to the temptation to nourish his legend, or accept his picture as reality. I pity the man who falls in love with his image as it is drawn by public opinion...."
{"Markings," by Dag Hammarskjold, New York: Alfred A. Knopf, 1964, p.66}

...Such is how *"popes"* on both sides of the pulpit are made. God deliver us from becoming such...beginning with me!

Yours in *"the fellowship of His sufferings,"*
The Broken Pastor!

CHAPTER 5

EFFECTIVE PREACHING NEEDS FAITHFUL PASTORING

"Like the coolness of snow at harvest time is a trustworthy messenger to those who send him; he refreshes the spirit of his masters."
[Proverbs 25:13]

What a simple but striking picture the Wise Teacher paints in Proverbs 25:13. Like the longed-for and welcomed, when it comes, cool, thirst-parching refreshment on a hot summer's day in the midst of the hard work of the harvest, so is the faithful messenger to both the recipients and the senders in what he has been trusted to carry. This proverb holds true for both the faithful pastor and the effective preacher.

The False Choice?

The great violinist, Georges Enesco, as a favour, agreed to teach his friend's son. Three years later the boy's father insisted that he give a public concert. Against his better judgement Enesco arranged the recital at the Salle Gaveau in Paris. No-one bought a ticket, however, because the soloist was unknown. *"Then you must accompany him on the piano and it will be a sell out!"* said the boy's father. Again, Enesco found himself reluctantly agreeing. On the night an excited audience had gathered. Enesco had become very nervous and asked for someone to turn his pages. In the audience was the brilliant pianist, Alfred Cortot, who volunteered and made his way to the stage. Unfortunately, the concert lived down to Enesco's feared low standard. The next morning the music critic of *"Le Figaro"* wrote: *"There was a strange concert at the Salle Gaveau last night. The man whom we adore when he plays the violin played the piano. Another whom we adore when he plays the piano turned the pages. But the man who should have turned the pages played the violin.*" {taken from "*The Book Of Heroic Failures*," by Stephen Pile. Futura Publications, c.1979, p.118}

If the truth be told there are many who feel that way about how things are done in the ministry of the Church, in particular in the ministry to the Church in terms of preaching and pastoring. There are many pastors who are not preachers and many preachers who will not pastor – we need to be honest about that, because the people to whom we are sent already know it. In the Denomination I grew up in and subsequently pastored in for many years, pastoral ministry had become quite rigid and thus limited – pastors were not only expected to pastor but to preach, with the result being the Church equivalent of that awkward night at the Salle Gaveau! This was common – and still is in some parts – across many denominations, contributing in the heritage of the pastor being the *"one man band"* while the congregation, largely, looks on from the sidelines of the pew. Undoubtedly, in the last twenty-five to thirty years, many parts of the Church have been emerging from this *"monster"* of ministry, getting back to the Scriptural *"model"* for ministry of the likes of 1 Corinthians 12 and Ephesians 4 where the Church is not a *"one man band"* but a *"body"* looking to each part to find its place and play its part:

"Now to each one the manifestation of the Spirit is given for the common good....The body is a unit, though it is made up of many parts; and though all its parts are many, they form one body. So it is with Christ." [1 Corinthians 12:7 & 12]

"...It was [Christ] *Who gave some to be apostles, some to be prophets, some to be evangelists, and some to be pastors and teachers, to prepare God's people for works of service, so that the body of Christ may be built up"* [Ephesians 4:11-12]

Without, in any way, seeking to disregard this or send us back into the *"ministry-muddle"* we have still yet to fully break free from, I do want to submit to the reader this contention: faithful pastors do not need to preach but effective preachers do need to pastor! A pastor should not be expected to preach – there is a genuine and even good *"choice"* here. But the preacher who will not pastor – this is a *"false choice."*

I am sure we have all heard the quip about the pastor who is *"invisible all week and incomprehensible on Sunday!"* That's what happens, even to the best, when we become cloistered in our study with our books but distant from the people in the pew! Whereas, it is true that on a Sunday, through the sermon, the people I pastor will indirectly get to know how I have been spending my time, the pulpit must never become a platform for *"self"* where I can con people with my cleverness – to do so is to be a con because, in pointing to self, I no longer am a means of *"refreshment",* instead, I have become an unfaithful *"messenger."* Those of us who work hard and honestly in the place of study will oftentimes have to restrict ourselves in taking all the information we have into the pulpit with us – to overload with information can become a distraction, whereby we sabotage the very message we have been entrusted to proclaim. Dr. Billy Graham has testified that there are many subjects and messages he would have loved to preach but has had to *"restrict"* himself in doing so because his calling is to be an *"evangelist,"* and thus, there needs to be a certain direction and content to his preaching which does not allow him to preach in other ways over other things. He has been a faithful and *"refreshing messenger."* A great part of his ministry also involves being with people. Sadly, there have been many other evangelists who come to Churches and are insensitive to the people who would hear them, because they have allowed their direction of ministry – travelling – to separate them from people in general. Are not the best evangelists those who have, at some point, served in the pastoral situation of the local Church? Again, I commend Dr. Graham in this regard.

Those of us who are called to preach must know and remind ourselves and help the congregation come to understand that pastoral preaching is not strictly the same as evangelistic preaching – and there must be a place for conscious evangelistic preaching in the preaching schedule of the local Church – and neither is pastoral preaching the same as Bible Study, and preaching must never be confused with speech-making or lecturing!

A pastor may not be a preacher – and should neither be automatically expected to be and thus forced into such. But the preacher who wants to be effective does not have the *"luxury"* of such a *"choice"* – if he is going to preach in a way that will *"refresh"*, he needs, not only, to know where his hearers are but he must also go to where they are. The footsteps of the preacher must go through his parish on the way from the study to the pulpit and back again.

Restoring The Sacredness Of Pastoral Visitation!

As I write this, I think of a pastoral colleague who would be cheering at what has been written above. He is a pastor – for him, study and preaching are hard things, even unwelcome to him. He would say to me, *"I was feeling down and so I went and did some pastoral visits!"* I am the other way. I am primarily a preacher and because of that I know I need to be a pastor. However, because of where my calling and gifting and burden is – preaching – and the time I need to give to it if I am going to be faithful in it, then how and where I spend my time becomes a pressing issue. How many pastors honestly believe that when it comes to the expectations and demands of pastoral visitation their time could be better spent?

"Mrs. Huff is up the miff tree
On a seat fixed good and firm;
And she'd like to tell the pastor
A few things to make him squirm.

Mrs. Huff was sick abed, sir,
Yes, sir, sick abed a week!
And the pastor didn't call, sir,
Never even took a peek.

When I asked her if the doctor
Called to see her, she said, 'Sure!'
And she looked as if she thought I
Needed some good mental cure.

Then I asked her how the doctor
Knew that sickness laid her low,
And she said that she had called him
On the 'phone and told him so.

Now the doctor gets his bill paid
With a nicely written cheque;
But the pastor, for not knowing,
Simply gets it in the neck!"
{Anonymous}

What pastor does not know a *"Mrs. Huff and her miff tree"*? Indeed, such can make us want to retreat to our studies and lock ourselves away!

There is a need to restore the sacredness of the Pastoral Visit – many parishioners abuse it, thinking it is their right – *"What else do we pay him for?"* – and like Mrs. Huff think the pastor should be there at their *"beck and call"* over anything! On the other hand, many pastors have abused the sacredness of the Pastoral Visit, allowing it to degenerate into nothing more than a social visit. This, alone, has gone a long way to creating the stereotypical image of the pastor who *"works one day a week and spends the rest of his time visiting old ladies, drinking tea and eating cake!"* The evident poor preparation for a Sunday and an expanding waistline does nothing to allay the conclusion many have arrived at regarding pastors and how hard they actually work and what they do with their time.

If we are to be faithful pastors, restoring the sacredness of the *"visit"* then there are some things we may like to consider:
- Unless you are visiting over a specific critical issue, twenty minutes in a home is more than enough, and even less for a hospital visit.
- Politely refuse tea and food, or, at least, restrict yourself to perhaps taking a drink in only one visit per day.
- By all means, CONNECT with those who you are visiting – talking about sport, keeping up with the other family members, who they are,

what they are doing, etc – but at some point, the pastor needs to ask after the soul(s) of the one(s) he is visiting. If such does not come up in the course of conversation, the pastor should bring it up. Before leaving, this pastor always prays, and kneels to pray. This is not a gimmick, but it has a profound effect on a home, by a hospital bed.

• Record the date and time of every pastoral visit. We will, subtly but surely, tend towards people we have a natural affinity with. One of the most challenging aspects of ministry is to be a faithful pastor to those who do not want you to be the pastor – some who make no attempt to hide the fact – but we still have to pastor them. Keeping a record of pastoral visitation will help ensure that we cover all who are under our care.

• This pastor, generally, will not visit those who are under the care of another pastor. There are those in the Church who just want to be surrounded by pastors. Duplicating pastoral care is an unwise use of time not to mention an unhelpful encouragement of spiritually immature, if not carnal, behaviour.

Pastoral Visitation should be a sacred event and not a social activity – we dishonour God and do a disservice to those we care for to allow it to be otherwise. I intentionally set the above in a pointed manner, not to be dogmatic, but to help encourage the reader to think.

Four Steps To Guarding The Sacredness Of The Pulpit!
This *"guarding"* begins with the pastor in his own heart. The Wise Teacher counsels: *"Above all else, GUARD your heart...."* [Proverbs 4:23] One of the greatest dangers to befall a preacher is when he starts to only open God's Book to get a sermon for others. The preacher's personal devotional life with God should never be confused or substituted for his study preparation in preaching. On occasions there will be a happy and wise overflow from one into the other but there is a fundamental difference and this needs to be recognized, respected and maintained.

The second step in guarding the sacredness of the pulpit is in regard to how the preacher spends his time. Without dismantling the argument that has already been made – that Effective Preaching Needs Faithful Pastoring

– the preacher needs to *"guard"* his study time. The preacher/pastor is not a taxi service, nor a furniture remover, nor a social worker, nor a general all round dogsbody and handy-man! When the preacher/pastor becomes too easily accessible he is affirming the popular opinion that he does not really do *"proper"* work anyway and so his time is not really precious because he is always available! Remember Martin Luther's costly personal lesson in Chapter 3.

Step three is an argument for Series Preaching! If the Bible is the *"whole counsel of God"* then we should preach from it all in that knowledge – series preaching is a great aid to that. It keeps us balanced, saving us from the soapbox preaching of our *"pet"* issues. I would humbly suggest that the healthiest diet a preacher/pastor can give a congregation is the regime of series preaching. Such not only stretches the preacher in that it forces him to remain a student in the Scriptures, but it also deepens the knowledge and enlarges appreciation of the congregation as to the whole of Scripture. Apart from anything else, it relieves the pastor from that terrible *"Monday morning feeling"* of sitting at his desk with a blank sheet of paper, desperately wondering what he is going to preach on next Sunday! Series preaching helps protect against the accusation that we are *"preaching AT"* instead of *"preaching TO"*. If there is a contentious issue and we just jump in and out of nowhere start preaching about it then we could be open to the charge of abusing the pulpit, but if, for example, that contentious issue is addressed in a New Testament Letter we are preaching through, it comes up to be dealt with naturally and transparently honestly. Series preaching needs one important qualification – it is a great method but should never be a master. There will be times and places because there is a need, because of a situation, or a *"timing"* from Heaven, for the *"landmark"* sermon. We need to be flexible enough to change our plans, always being sensitive to what the *"*[Holy] *Spirit says to the churches…."* [Revelation 2:7] Both preachers and congregations need anointed hearing.

The final step of this particular quartet regards the preacher/pastoral responsibility, not only of what is preached – ie: Scripture – but also of who is allowed to preach. The pulpit ministry should never be unthinkingly open to all-comers. Not everyone who can preach should preach – this calls for discernment. Not every one who wants to preach can preach and should therefore be allowed to preach – this calls for diplomacy! This saves the whole Church ministry from falling victims to the same kind of farce that took place at the Salle Gaveau. This is an important, even urgent, matter that needs to be worked out in every local Church. I guess the word is *"INTEGRITY"*! A commitment to honour the Master of the message!

The Final Word On Pastoral Ministry – *"PRESENCE!"*

Over the years the congregations who hear us preach may not remember much, if any, of all we have preached to them – but they will thankfully remember our *"PRESENCE"* in those crisis times when life fell apart on them. Job's three friends get a lot of bad press, but we often forget that for the first seven days they got it absolutely right: *"...they sat on the ground with [Job] for seven days and seven nights. No one said a word to him, because they say how great his suffering was"* [Job 2:13]. In those times and places in life there is nothing to be said, nothing we can say, and those whom we pastor know that. The pressure we feel to have to break the silence of suffering and bring some kind of *"sense"* and meaning to it springs from the sense of our own insecure-inability in that situation, and even our own pride. We cannot *"speak"* hurt away – we must, however, stay where hurt is until it begins to subside. Those we pastor are not listening to our words as much as they are looking to lean on our faithful, silent *"presence."* This is why *"Effective Preaching Needs Faithful Pastoring!"*

Yours in the *"fellowship of His sufferings,"*
The Broken Pastor!

CHAPTER 6

EXPECTATIONS

"…we had hoped…." [Luke 24:21]

On his first parachute jump a soldier received the following instructions from his sergeant: *"You count to ten and then pull this cord. If the parachute fails you pull the emergency parachute cord here. And then try to land near the lorry down there – they will have a nice cup of tea waiting for you."* The parachutist does what he is told - counts to ten and pulls the cord….Nothing happens. He then pulls the emergency cord….Nothing happens. As he hurtles towards the lorry he is heard to mutter, *"I bet there's no cup of tea either!"*

How many Pastors, along with the two on the Emmaus Road who first spoke them, have also uttered these words as they wearily trudge along in ministry? Still walking and talking and giving - but walking away from their dreams, talking down their prospects, giving up on the promise – *"…we had hoped..."*? Like the disillusioned parachutist, many leave Bible College and/ or enter ministry with such high hopes only to descend into disappointment, with no hopeful outlook remaining for even the most basic of positive outcomes, like our equivalent *"cup of tea"*! The *"honeymoon"* is over, even short-lived, and reality takes over. And it is not nice. What did we expect from our *"Expectations"*?

Disappointed *"Expectations"* - Not The Fate Of The Half-Hearted!
"…we had hoped…." – who would speak words like that? Not the half-hearted, for whom following Jesus is a hobby, a far-off, shallow thing, always stopping short in the giving of self, never reaching the cross.

Such expressions of lost hope and dashed *"Expectations"* are not sinful, and neither are those from whom they come, failures – there is one reading these words and you really need to know that! It's the committed who have dreams. It's disciples who have a cause. *"...we had hoped...."* – these words betray not only disappointment but also devotion. Did these two only hear about the death of Jesus on the cross or did they witness it themselves? Was it not what they had seen for themselves at the cross of Jesus, and not just heard about from others, that made their sense of loss so deep, compelling them to leave Jerusalem? In reading the wider account of this incident the New International Version titles, *"On The Road To Emmaus"* [Luke 24:13-35], there is a very real sense in which this pair knew what they were talking about in regard to the event of Christ's crucifixion – these men had actually been there at the cross of Jesus, seeing it all for themselves. They didn't just *"hear"* – they *"knew"* for sure. It took devotion to do that – to go to the cross of Jesus, and stay there, watching Him die, until, as far as they are concerned, it's over – *"...we had hoped...."* If there was no devotion to the Saviour then there would have been no real and deep disappointment when He was seen to die on a cross, taking all their hopes with Him.

For us, on the *"other side"* of the cross of Jesus, in the light of His resurrection, even with *"burning hearts within us,"* does God on a cross still not remain so hard, even impossible, to understand? The cross in all it stands for, will always be a cruel place – unfair and wasteful and perplexingly so. What survives beyond a cross where we know what we saw, because we were there – expectations dashed... *"HOPE"* DIE? What do we do, where do we go, what does it mean for us when *"Expectation"* is crucified on the cross of reality – not just wounded, but slain...killed...and all we had worked for... given ourselves to – *"...we had hoped..."*? The chances are that the faithful one who may be reading this finds himself taking a walk he would never have believed because of what has happened. *"Expectation"* has taken one *"hit"* too many. Many of us *"Broken Pastors"*, like the broken disciples on the Emmaus Road, are still walking – but away!...Still talking – but down!...Still giving – but up! *"...we had hoped...."*

Living In Contradiction!

Not long after entering the pastorate I came across this insightfully humorous piece titled, *"Vision And Reality"*:

EXPECTATION – never take a Church unless it extends you a unanimous call.
REALITY – never take a Church unless it extends you a call.

EXPECTATION – never take a Church unless you are willing to stay there for the rest of your life.
REALITY – don't bail out unless you've stuck it out for at least two years.

EXPECTATION – only you are on the payroll, not your spouse. The congregation has no right to place expectations on your spouse.
REALITY – make sure your spouse never misses Church, is President of the Missionary Society and is a Sunday School teacher.

EXPECTATION – recruit only dedicated, visionary Christians to serve on the Church Board.
REALITY – recruit only Christians to serve on the Church Board.

EXPECTATION – immerse your ministry in prayer.
REALITY – immerse your ministry in prayer and administration.

EXPECTATION – spend an hour in study for each minute in the pulpit.
REALITY – spend at least one hour preparing your sermon.

EXPECTATION – don't wait until Saturday night to prepare your sermon.
REALITY – don't wait until Sunday morning to prepare your sermon.

EXPECTATION – always preach your convictions without regard for the consequences.
REALITY – suss out the Church Board members on controversial matters to know what convictions to preach.

EXPECTATION – don't neglect your family.
REALITY – don't neglect the Church Board.

EXPECTATION – take a day off every week.
REALITY – take a day off every month.

EXPECTATION – don't mess with the Ladies' Group.
REALITY – don't mess with the Ladies' Group!

{"Vision & Reality" – source unknown}

Pastors young and old, new and experienced, will not only be able to relate to, but will also have some of their own compiled lists of *"Vision And Reality"*! Every pastor who comes into the ministry has *"Expectations"* – expectations as to what ministry in a local Church will be like, expectations as to what he will do and how he will go about it, expectations of a salary and accommodation, expectations of the congregation and how he will serve them and how they will support him in working together, expectations of cooperation. We thank God that *"as far as the east is from the west, so far has He removed our transgressions from us"* [Psalm 103:12] but there are times when the gulf between high *"Expectations"* and low, even loathsome, reality, to us feels very wide, undiminished, and therefore, unable to be reconciled. Contradiction is very hard to live with. Neither the world in which we live, or the people we serve in it, including ourselves, are perfect. We live in an atmosphere of contradiction. Romans 8:22 speaks of the *"whole creation... groaning"* – what is this *"groaning"* but the testimony to contradiction? God will not only bring resolution to every contradiction in the fullness of His time, but in the meantime, He works in the midst of our contradictions, working His purposes out through them. The whole Incarnation event was an exercise in glorious contradiction. Charles Wesley inspirationally captured it – *"Our God contracted to a span, Incomprehensibly made man"* {*"Let Earth And Heaven Combine,"* by Charles Wesley, verse 1} – a magnificent contradiction. In Romans 4:17 the Bible speaks of the salvation-activity of God in humanity – *"...the God Who gives life to the dead and calls things that are not as though they were"* – what a stunning contradiction! In Romans 8:21 and 23 Paul tells us that the creation *"groans…in hope of liberation"* even in *"eager"* anticipation of *"adoption"* and *"redemption"*. Indeed, is it not this in-between place of conflict, where we *"wait"* for our resolution and reconciliation, that makes the contradiction so hard to bear, where we sometimes wonder and often flag – *"…we had hoped…"*?

Understanding The *"Rights"* And Limits Of Our *"Expectations"*!

Just like there were some things the duo on the Emmaus Road had to learn and come to understand about the *"…we had hoped…"* of the Saviour and the cross, there are also things we have to learn and understand about the *"…we had hoped…"* of service and the cross. Jesus not only had *"Expectations"* and understood His *"rights"* but also what do with them, especially when they are rubbished and not realized in reality. The question is – *"DO WE HAVE A RIGHT TO OUR EXPECTATIONS IN THE SERVICE OF GOD?"* Could *"Expectation"* even be part of our sinful flesh needing to be crucified?

If we take a look at how Jesus prepared His disciples for ministry we see that He seems to go out of His way to destroy illusions, dash expectations, even setting His disciples up for disappointment and self-denial in the face of these difficult realities. For example:

• *"Take nothing for the journey except a staff – no bread, no bag, no money in your belts. Wear sandals but not an extra tunic. Whenever you enter a house, stay there until you leave that town. And if any place will not welcome you or listen to you, shake the dust off your feet when you leave, as a testimony against them"* [Mark 6:8-11].

• *"If the world hates you, keep in mind that it hated Me first….Remember the words I spoke to you: 'No servant is greater than his master.' If they persecuted Me, they will persecute you also….They will put you out of the synagogue; in fact, a time is coming when anyone who kills you will think he is offering a service to God"* [John 15:18 & 20 & 16:2].

• *"I tell you the truth, when you were younger you dressed yourself and went where you wanted; but when you are old you will stretch out your hands, and someone else will dress you and lead you where you do not want to go.... Follow Me!"* [John 21:18-19]

What is Jesus saying here but, *"You are not going to make a lot of money and gain a lot of worldly prestige when you serve Me. You are not to be treated like kings. You are not to pursue promotion. Don't look for ways to advance self interest. You will not always be welcomed and understood and appreciated. Indeed, some of those you seek to serve the most and who should know better, will repay you with the worst. In following Me you are to deny self - not pamper self; give your life - not protect and even prolong your life! Your 'expectations' will be crucified, over and over again!"*

This was the reality, not only of the first disciples. The Apostle Paul wrote:
"For it seems to me that God has put us apostles on display at the end of the procession, like men condemned to die in the arena. We have been made a spectacle to the whole universe, to angels as well as to men. We are fools for Christ, but you are so wise in Christ! We are weak, but you are strong! You are honoured, we are dishonoured! To this very hour we go hungry and thirsty, we are in rags, we are brutally treated, we are homeless. We work hard with our own hands. When we are cursed, we bless; when we are persecuted, we endure it; when we are slandered, we answer kindly. Up to this moment we have become the scum of the earth, the refuse of the world" [1 Corinthians 4:9-13].

Now, in many ways, we would expect this treatment from the *"world,"* but here in his first letter to the Corinthians Paul is writing to Christ-ones and contrasting himself and his fellow apostles, not with the world that would resist them, but with some in the Church who were opposing them and *"questioning"* their authenticity. When that happens, from your *"own"*, those who do know better, dashed *"Expectations"* are so very hard to bear, and the urge to reconcile the contradiction, even through walking away, talking down, and giving up, becomes more pressing.

Rob Parsons preached a powerful sermon that was also a book he wrote, *"Bringing Home The Prodigals."* He says: *"You and I do not have the right to belong to a church that suits us in every respect. The great tragedy of much of church life today is that we have come to believe that 'church is for us'… [I]n our hearts we have a view of what suits us and woe betide the leadership if we don't get it…."* {"Bringing Home The Prodigals," by Rob Parsons, c.2003. Published by Hodder & Stoughton, p.81}.

How much do we see of this in the life of the Church? However, if, in the above quote, we were to substitute the words *"church"* for *"ministry"* and the word *"leadership"* for *"congregation"*, we would arrive at the reality of misunderstanding too many in the pastorate have of their *"rights",* including their rights to have certain *"Expectations"* met – pastors who expect their congregations to always fall in line and *"serve"* them, for their benefit, from their egos to their comforts! Pastors who will not go to a certain church because the numbers are low, the salary is not enough, the accommodation is below standard. I am not suggesting that these things do not matter nor condoning a Church being negligent in its responsibility of care to the pastor, what I am contending is that these should not regulate, in either stipulation or negation, a call of God to service. If we will not serve unless certain conditions/*"Expectations"* are met then how can we reconcile it in the following of the One Who left the glory of Heaven for the dust of the earth, Who took on the flesh of humanity in submitting Himself as a foetus in a human womb for nine months, was born in a stable, had no possessions, was crucified, coming to His *"own"* who would neither recognize or receive Him [John 1:11]? In the light of Him, I need to Understand My *"Rights"*…that even my *"rights"* to *"Expectations"* are to be left at the cross of Jesus, especially when they are not fulfilled.

Resentment Or Abandonment?

In 2 Corinthians 1:8-9, the Apostle Paul writes of being, *"…under great pressure, far beyond our ability to endure, so that we despaired even of life. Indeed, in our hearts we felt the sentence of death…."* And when our hearts are heavy and weary from disappointed *"Expectations"*, we do feel *"the sentence of death"*, it is hard to bear. These things are unfair. I hate it when the Church that pays me has *"Expectations"* of my wife who is called by God to be my wife and not a *"pastor's wife"*! It pains me to see the *"Expectations"* many in Churches put on pastors' children, who never had a choice about being born into a manse (parsonage) family, but who are forced to bear the burden of it nonetheless. In regard to *"Expectations"* what faithful pastor has not *"felt the sentence of death"* when they are not met? Whereas the two on the Emmaus Road walked away from the cross, *"...we had hoped...."*, the Apostle Paul took his despair to the cross. He continues in 2 Corinthians 1:9: *"...But this happened that we might not rely on ourselves but on God, Who raises the dead."*

We do not have a *"right"*, even a right to hold on to our *"Expectations."* What Parsons says is true of the whole Church, but if it is ever going to be, it needs to begin by being modelled by pastors and leaders, in the denial of self, the abandonment of self, not to the keeping of the Church in my *"Expectations"* of them and theirs' of me, but to the keeping of God, Who always leads us to and through a cross. It is the cross that takes us beyond the continued life of self and into the consecrated life of Christ, Who laid aside His *"rights"* – His *"right"* to His Self and the satisfying of *"Expectations"* -and Who did not stop and walk away at the limit of His *"Expectations"*. Walking away from the cross with our disappointed *"Expectations"* ultimately leads to resentment. Leaving my broken *"Expectations"* at the cross can only lead to abandonment – my total self, surrendered, in trusting-identification with Him!

In his book, *"The Importance Of Being Foolish - How To Think Like Jesus,"* Brennan Manning writes of how *"self"* is liberated when we no longer look to the surface issues of life and living, including other people, for our sense of meaning, worth, and security:

"...We experience everyone and everything around us in a different way – not in terms of how they meet our needs ['Expectations']....We live in rhythm with the mind of Christ Jesus and enter into the flow and harmony of God's creative design... In Jesus there was no self to be seen, only the ultimate, unconditional love of God...." {"The Importance Of Being Foolish," by Brennan Manning, Harper Collins Publishers, c.2005, pp.94-95}

What is Manning saying but that beyond our *"Expectations"*, better than our *"Expectations"*, and greater than our broken *"Expectations"* is the unconditional love of God and the unchangeableness of our belonging to Him? And thus, when *"Expectations"* die, as they will, *"...we had hoped...."* is replaced by, *"...we are forever loved...!"* And YOU are FOREVER LOVED!

Yours in *"the fellowship of His sufferings,"*
The Broken Pastor!

CHAPTER 7

THE HAUNTING ISSUE OF CHURCH BUSINESS

"Let all things be done decently and in order."
[1 Corinthians 14:40, K.J.V.]

A young, new pastor was talking to one of the longest standing Board Members in the Church. This man had served continuously for over forty years. This *"green"* pastor was amazed at such a record, he said to the elderly Church statesman, *"You must have seen a lot of changes in those forty years!"* To which came the immediate, sharp reply, *"Yes, and I have opposed every one of them!"*

Church Business Meetings have become *"Haunting Issues"* for many in the Church – on both sides of the pulpit! From committee meetings, to regular Board meetings, to the general meetings of the Church, the way the business of the Church has been approached and applied has been the source of many painful memories, leaving a decidedly bitter taste – even bad taste – in the mouth, which can linger for years, with some never getting rid of it and thus never getting over it. Time and again, the Church Business Meeting has been anything but the *"finest hour"* for a local Church, but rather has seen Churches split and pastors quit. Such occasions have been used to settle *"scores"*, to pursue hidden agendas. Pastors have been voted out of their Churches by the action of a Church meeting, which was not the will of the wider Church, but the contributing factors of bad weather, illness among the congregation, and even the short-notice in announcing the meeting, led to many not being able to attend, and so vital votes, which would otherwise have ensured the pastor's protection and continuance, were not able to be placed. On the flimsy basis of bad weather, unforeseen circumstance, and inconvenience, the course of many local Churches and the fate of many pastors has been unfairly decided, with the consequences coming to haunt for years to come.

No matter the size of the local Church, or the form of Church Government, there is always room for the loaded question, the *"red-herring"* issue, the influential but still fleshly voice of just *"one"* individual who can sway and manipulate the course, not only of a comparatively small committee meeting, but even a whole Church business meeting, ultimately to the detriment of all. This is why many pastors, including the one writing, have gone to monthly Church board meetings with their stomachs in knots, and before the Annual Business Meetings of the Church, can lose sleep for many nights before, and end up losing their homes afterwards. How many *"good"* people have left the Church, damaged and injured, because of the care which was not taken with the business of the Church? Having enough stress to deal with in the workplace and in the home, without needing it in the Church, they reach a limit, and, for their own survival, have to walk away. Time and again, it is the best people we lose, while the *"animals"* remain and are allowed to take over the *"zoo-bedlam"* the Church has become, or the inmates allowed to run the *"asylum of insanity"* the church has descended into – take your pick, neither of these metaphors is an overstatement or oversimplification! For too many it has become *"The Haunting Issue of Church Business!"*

...However, it does not need to be this way; even now it is not too late!

Worship Is The *"Business"* Of The Church!

"Let all things be done decently and in order." The context of the Apostle Paul's concluding admonition of 1 Corinthians 14 is worship. To apply these same words to the specific issue of the Church's *"business"* is neither to take them out of their initial context nor to stretch it. This pastor would contend, because the Scriptures clearly show it, that our *"business,"* whether it be of our daily lives or our corporate lives in the Church, is to be seen as an act of worship. For the child of God, there is no distinction between the *"sacred"* and

the *"secular"* – to the one who belongs to God, all of life is *"sacred"*, because all of life comes from the hand of God and lived at and for His *"pleasure"* [Revelation 4:11, K.J.V.]. We are always stewards unto Him, never owners unto ourselves.

In the realm of our individual lives we are told:

"Wives, submit to your husbands, as is fitting in the Lord.
Husbands, love your wives and do not be harsh with them.
Children, obey your parents in everything, for this pleases the Lord.
Fathers, do not embitter your children, or they will become discouraged.
Slaves, obey your earthly masters in everything; and do it, not only when their eye is on you and to win their favour, but with sincerity of heart and reverence for the Lord. Whatever you do, work at it with all your heart, as working for the Lord, not for men, since you know that you will receive an inheritance from the Lord as a reward. It is the Lord Christ you are serving...."
[Colossians 3:18-24]

When it came to the *"business"* of choosing His first Disciples, the Bible tells us that Jesus spent a whole night in prayerful preparation [Luke 6:12ff]. What would happen to and in the *"business"* of the Church, whatever its format, if those participating came to the meeting having spent a night in prayerful preparation before God?

When it came to the *"business"* of the early Church, they were able to write this account: *"...it seemed good to the Holy Spirit and to us..."* [Acts 15:28]. What needs to happen for such to be recorded in the minutes of how it was, in what took place in the business of our meetings?

My personal preparation for a business meeting – my truthfulness in what I report, my carefulness in what I say, my attitude in how I relate and react, my motives in what I do and how and why I seek to do it – are as much a part of my worship to God as is my praying and Bible reading and singing and witnessing and serving. Always, in every thing *"...It is the Lord Christ you are serving"* [Colossians 3:24].

However, we must not be so foolish to suggest and suppose that just because we come to say such things about the *"business"* of the Church, surrounding it with the right words, calling it *"worship"*, that it will then automatically be. We have a responsibility to make it so....

The Limits Of *"Democracy"*!

No matter what form of *"government"* a Church may subscribe to, there is a need for all to recognize that there are limits to democracy within the Church. In the Church of God, *"democracy"* can never be the first word or the final word – in all things, primarily and ultimately, the Church is not a democracy, but a *"Theocracy"*. We come under the rule of God first (*"Theocracy"*), and only ever in a secondary manner should we be taken up with the rights of our democracy. The Church of God has never been a *"free for all"* in terms of who leads – and it is our failure to recognize this that has led to much of our sorry history in this regard! Because of the sinfulness of the human heart, we live in a world where neither *"might"* nor the majority is always right. The *"freedom"* of our actions and the *"rights"* of our decisions need the guidance of God, because we all ultimately need to be guarded against ourselves: *"The heart is deceitful above all things and beyond cure. Who can understand it?"* [Jeremiah 17:9] And that remains the dangerous potential, even of the *"redeemed heart"*, which still lives within a fallen body, in a fallen, still yet to be redeemed, world. The Church problems confronted in most of the New Testament Letters testify to this.

We do well to remind ourselves that one of the earliest recorded business meetings of God's people was a catastrophic failure, because it was carried out on the basis of democracy, from beginning to end. I refer to the twelve Moses sent to spy out the land of Canaan, on the basis of what God had said (Theocracy). But the Bible tells us the recommendation on their return – by a vote of *"10 to 2"* – was that they could never possibly take this land of promise. Democracy won the day, the consequences of which were suffered for a generation. Numbers 13:32 refers to it as a *"bad report"* – how many bad votes and bad decisions have been made by virtue of a *"bad report"* with devastating results over many years?

One of the most important *"elections"* of the New Testament was at the end of Acts 1 in choosing a replacement to succeed Judas [Acts 1:21-26]. We are told that a test/criteria was laid out, that they proposed two names, that they prayed, and that they *"cast lots, and the lot fell to Matthias."* Let this writer suggest to the reader something to consider (which is, in no way, a conclusion): did the Church get this election right? I ask that because after Acts 1:26 neither *"casting lots"* in regard to the electing to Church leadership, nor *"Matthias"* are ever mentioned again? Could this, like the debacle at Kadesh (Numbers 13), be another warning as to the quickly reached Limits Of Democracy?

We need to recognize God's right to His *"Theocracy,"* seeing the rights of our democracy within that. In both Old and New Testaments, there are clear instructions and procedures God sets out as to the choices of leadership and service:

• God told Gideon, in regard to the assembling of the initial army to take on the Midianites: *"…Take them down to the water, and I will sift them for you there. If I say, 'This one shall go with you,' he shall go; but if I say, 'This one shall not go with you,' he shall not go"* [Judges 7:4]. If we read on we see that God set out certain tests, a framework, for establishing who should be selected and who should not be. Being a willing, ever-present *"fixture"* in Church attendance, does not in itself warrant suitability for being chosen to serve in leadership. We need to *"see"* how people conduct themselves as to their spiritual awareness.

• In Acts 6, those who were *"chosen"* to *"wait on tables"* were those *"known to be full of the Spirit and wisdom"* [Acts 6:2-3] – how much more the leadership of the Church? But again, note how even the basic tasks of *"waiting on tables"* was seen through the eyes of genuine and proved spirituality, as an act of worship and service to God.

• Perhaps the clearest Theocratic boundaries, inside which our democracy must fit, come in Paul's First Letter to Timothy – 1 Timothy 3. God sets the boundaries, outlines the tests – such is the rule of His Theocracy – then, and only after then, and always according to, may we employ and enjoy the rights of our democracy.

Safety In *"Numbers"*!

By *"Numbers"* I don't mean the strength of a vote, or the *"spinning"* of statistics, but rather the orderly keeping of the pastor's work, especially in regard to pastoral visitation. A pastor can go a long way in protecting himself if he is a good organizer, seeking to be transparent, having as much information he can at his disposal. Whilst it is generally and rightly understood that much of a pastor's work, especially in the area of counselling, must be confidential, it needs to be confessed that we pastors have sometimes been guilty of hiding behind claimed *"confidentiality"* as an excuse for our tardiness in lack of preparation and punctuality, covering our tawdriness. Much of what we are engaged in must, and can, be open to examination and question.

I remember one particular Annual Business Meeting – which will last long in the memory, sadly – and quite a significant group who had not been to Church for months, turned up, to try and derail the meeting, taking the clear opportunity such meetings tend to allow, to cleverly *"attack"* the pastor, through the decoy of the privileges of the democratic process. One of the *"group"* stood up and announced his disquiet at the performance of the pastor in specific regard to his visitation. Going on to say that in the nine months he had not been in attendance at Church the pastor had not even visited him once. In response to this, I reached behind me and brought out a large file – my *"Pastoral Visitation"* file – located his name, and was able to calmly correct him and reassure the wider congregation that I had visited his home on three different occasions in that period, citing the relevant dates, and also the other instances when a visit had been attempted but there was no-one at home. The man quietly sat down, no longer having any *"leg"* to stand on – the *"gust"* suddenly taken out of his sails! This simple habit of recording my visits – when and who – helps protect against such accusations of pastoral negligence, which are often nothing of the kind, but rather the shielded weapon of a personal vendetta.

Calling The *"Fouls"*!

No matter who we are, how old we are, what position we hold and experience and influence we have, not one of us is above being naughty and beyond being wrong. Like an umpire in sport, we too – pastor and congregation – need to *"Call the 'fouls'"*, putting a stop to inappropriate conduct, no matter who or where it is coming from. There was a situation in the early Church over which Peter was being inconsistent, manifesting a *"hidden agenda"*. Peter was regarded as the *"Senior Apostle"*, he had been around a lot longer than Paul, yet Paul writes in Galatians 2:11: *"When Peter came to Antioch, I opposed him to his face, because he was clearly in the wrong."* Too often we are silent to the *"face"* but verbal behind the *"back,"* in the *"safe"* environment of our own home – where is the worth in that, not to mention the honour and honesty? What is the point in complaining and having the courage of our convictions after the fact?

Is there not also something wrong when God's people justify their actions, applauding the bravery and wisdom of taking on a role which the world calls, *"devil's advocate"*? Why would we ever want to be associated with that? The very first *"loaded question"* that was ever recorded was on the lips of satan: *"Did God really say, ' You must not eat from any tree in the garden?'"* [Genesis 3:1] How many similar questions are found on the lips of professed Christ-ones in the business meetings of the Church? Is it not time to call *"foul"* and put a halt to it? Jesus said, *"Simply let your 'Yes' be 'Yes,' and your 'No,' 'No'; anything beyond this comes from the evil one"* [Matthew 5:37]. Such can never be defended and should therefore never be allowed.

In *"Defining Moments"* {c. & p. Willow Creek Association}, Pastor Bill Hybels of Willow Creek shares how their Church business meetings are carried out. Of particular relevance here is this practice of *"Calling the 'Fouls!'"* If an unhelpful comment is made, a mischievous question asked, a point of view aggressively expressed or ungraciously responded to, from either the front or the floor of the meeting, the rest of the Church quietly *"boo"* and *"hiss"* to show their disapproval. The *"foul"* has been called, and the relevant party/parties involved quickly admonished in a non-threatening but clear and effective way. Everybody – including the Pastor and leadership - is on the same learning curve, that will not defend nor allow such destructive behaviour, even if it is more of an impulsive moment than a malicious intention. The point is, we must not give ground in any way to the flesh – today's allowed momentary impulsiveness becomes tomorrow's accepted, even applauded, malicious intent. We need to establish a culture of *"zero tolerance"* in regard to these things.

In no way is the suggestion being made that there should never be differences of opinions aired, concerns expressed, tough, searching questions asked, and even criticisms made, but is there not something seriously wrong and urgently needing to be addressed when a pastor has to sit in a Church business meeting, with a Bible opened up in front of him at the likes of Isaiah 54:17 - *"'no weapon forged against you will prevail, and you will refute every tongue that accuses you. This is the heritage of the servants of the LORD, and this is their vindication from Me,' declares the LORD"* - as the agenda proceeds, in order to console himself and buoy his spirit in the face of crushing blows, malicious words, and vicious attacks from among those who call themselves the people of God?

Yours in *"the fellowship of His sufferings,"*
The Broken Pastor!

CHAPTER 8

THEM

"He had been hired to intimidate me…."
[Nehemiah 6:13]

…So noted Nehemiah, in the midst of a crucial work, about those who opposed him, seeking to *"intimidate"* him, using the dishonourable and thus demonic devices of unsubstantiated rumour – *"It is reported among the nations…"* [Nehemiah 6:6]; claimed but unconfirmed validation – *"…and Geshem says it is true…"* [Nehemiah 6:6]; false accusation – *"…that you… are plotting…"* [Nehemiah 6:6]; – carried in the *"unsealed letter"* [Nehemiah 6:5] for anyone and everyone who *"would"* to know and hear about, to create not only the public humiliation of the *"victim"*, but also to sow in Nehemiah's would-be protectors and supporters, seeds of suspicion and doubt: *"There must be something to it – people are talking about it; if Geshem is throwing his weight behind it…?; Perhaps Nehemiah isn't as trustworthy as we thought…?; and what about the public perception of unrest in the wider congregation…? Perhaps, for the sake of the wall and all, it is better to sacrifice Nehemiah? Geshem carries a lot of influence, and Sanballat and Tobiah have been around here a lot longer than Nehemiah!"* [see Nehemiah 2:10 & 19-20, Nehemiah 4 & 6]

How many pastors have become *"sacrificial lambs"* because of *"Them"*? Pushed out of their charges on the strength of the hot air of anonymous reports, from invisible sources, through, not only *"unsealed"* – for all to see - but often unsigned – for none to establish – letters. And thus, the *"wall"* never gets *"completed"*, because the *"wall-builder"* is no more. While the *"wall-wreckers"* remain, and what *"could have been"*, never is.

Who are these people? They are *"Them"*!

The Myth About *"Them"*!

It was during a particular low point, when being at the centre of a very public *"anti-pastor"* campaign in a local Church I served was taking a heavy personal toll, that a very kind and thoughtful parishioner passed on to me a little piece she had come across in a local prayer magazine, titled *"Them!"* {Source Unknown}. How true, when the pressure of an ever-increasing public attack mounts, *"Them"* are often quoted, cited, referred to, and, if we are not strong enough, believed and surrendered to.

"THEY say…!" *"SOME feel…!"* *"MANY will…!"* There are *"THOSE who…!"* Note – all threatening but anonymous…all having something to say but remaining unidentified…all expressing a concern, even making an accusation, but being unable to confirm…all tormenting the raw vulner-ability of a pastor, unhelpfully contributing to a dangerous paranoia, as they operate in the *"darkness"* and *"vagueness"* and *"aloofness"* of the *"RIGHT to CONFIDENTIALITY"* and *"PROTECTED ANONYMITY"* – refusing to come out in to the *"light"*.

What about the pastor's need for *"protection"* from unfair, because it is veiled, attack? What about the pastor's *"right"* to answer, not only the points of *"concern"*, but also the persons from whom they come? Why is it we hear about *"Them"* and feel their venom, but rarely get to see and meet *"Them"*? Is it because, most of the time, *"Them"* do not exist, but are used by 'Sanballat' and 'Tobiah' to strengthen their otherwise weak, minority, even personal, crusade, to sow suspicion by a misrepresentation to and of public opinion, to bring a veneer of *"credibility"* to their dishonourable behaviour?

"Them" can never be proved, because they never identify themselves, but neither can they be disputed, and such is the human heart in its tendency to latch on to the *"worst"* and the "bad," being easily panicked in the process, resulting in fear – satan knows that once you hear something, even if you don't believe it, you cannot un-hear it. Once something is suggested to you, again,

whether you accept it or not, awareness has been stirred, and even a perspective has been, unwillingly, perhaps, but at least, *"loaded"*, and even vitally altered. Words in this manner – written, spoken, and even unspoken in terms of a needful correction of the facts – are powerful in their destructiveness.

In this regard, because of how and who and where and when, *"Them"* operate like assassins do – undetected, in the shadows, striking from an unfair – to the 'target' – advantage, unleashing a fatal result. Have we forgotten that this is the kind of destructive behaviour God particularly abhors? He speaks against it in the strongest of terms. Proverbs tells us:

"A scoundrel and villain, who goes about with a corrupt mouth, who winks with his eye, signals with his feet and motions with his fingers, who plots evil with deceit in his heart – he always stirs up dissension. Therefore disaster will overtake him in an instant; he will suddenly be destroyed – without remedy.

There are six things the LORD hates, seven that are detestable to him: haughty eyes, a lying tongue, hands that shed innocent blood, a heart that devises wicked schemes, feet that are quick to rush into evil, a false witness who pours out lies and a man who stirs up dissension among brothers."

[Proverbs 6:12-19]

The Myth about *"Them"* – whether they be real or not, whether they be there or not – is that they are not WHO they say they are!

The Myth About *"US"*!

I use this term *"US"* guardedly. In many other contexts, to speak of *"Them"* and *"Us"* would be unwise because it is divisive. For our purposes here, we use it only as a reference point of definition in regard to what is, and also to how things can and should be.

The term *"Us"* specifically relates to the local Church Leadership, including the pastor. It is a *"myth"* to suggest and suppose that a Church Leadership is obligated to answer every *"letter"* that comes to it, address every *"issue"* that is raised, respond to every *"concern"* that is expressed and even *"accusation"* made. It is this pastor's contention that un-signed letters should not even be read, either privately, if addressed to an individual, or publicly, if addressed to a committee. The same would go for verbal but unsubstantiated quotes and *"confidential"* representations on behalf of , to all intents and purposes, invisible and unknown others - in terms of *"who?" "where?" "when?" "why?"* – because they are anonymous. Where is the honour in anonymity, especially among and between the people of God? If there does exist a genuine culture of *"fear of reprisal"* in the wider congregation for going on record over a matter, there are deeper-seated problems crying out to be addressed. On the main, this is not the case, rather, it is a cowardly way out, because it is carnally driven. The fact remains, if you can get a small group of people – anonymously or otherwise – to keep beating a certain drum, sending out a particular undercurrent message of discontent, without check, then there will always be enough who will, at least, believe some of it, without proof, thus giving *"Them"* a momentum of hearing and believing they do not merit, on the simple basis of that worldly proverb – *"There's no fire without some smoke!"*

In Nehemiah 6, an appeal is made to Nehemiah on the basis of *"the house of God"* [Nehemiah 6:10]. Some of the most vile letters a pastor will receive are not only *"unsealed"* and un-signed, but also quote Scripture throughout. Such is proof of nothing – if satan tried to intimidate and tempt even the Son of God to do evil, by quoting Scripture, how much more will the same be tried with us [see Luke 4:1-13]? We need to be wise and alert to these things. In his stirring book, *"Why Revival Tarries,"* Leonard Ravenhill submits, that in too much the Church believes the Bible to the point of inconvenience, then quits. Ravenhill wrote:

"One of these days some simple soul will pick up the Book of God, read it, and believe it. Then the rest of us will be embarrassed. We have adopted the convenient theory that the Bible is a Book to be explained, whereas first and foremost it is a Book to be believed (and after that to be obeyed)...."

{"Why Revival Tarries," by Leonard Ravenhill, c.1959, Bethany House Publishers, p.69}

...Oftentimes that *"embarrassment"* Ravenhill wrote of comes upon the wider Church Community when 'Nehemiah' finally stands up to the bullying tactics of the 'Sanballats" and 'Tobiahs", and does not get the needful support, because too many are more concerned about relieving their personal *"embarrassment"* and discomfort than acting decisively, courageously and selflessly for the *"common good"* [1 Corinthians 12:7ff], which as leaders we are called to protect and serve. Among other things, this responsibility of trust means holding on to 'Nehemiah' and facing down 'Sanballat' and 'Tobiah'. There are few things more frustrating and debilitating than leaders who will not lead, than those who love to *"parade"* their position but will not take on the fight from the front…and lead!

What are much of the New Testament Letters to the Church, but instructions on how we are to conduct ourselves as *"God's household"* [1 Timothy 3:15]? It is one thing, even an easier thing, to be applying the Scriptures, particularly to the open target the *"world"* is in its ignorant departure from the Word of God, but it is quite a different matter, and harder, when there is misbehaviour among and between *"God's household."* The Apostle Paul takes it even further, thus making it clearer, maintaining the theme of Biblical application in regard to the need for not only Church Instruction but also Church Discipline when there are serious departures: *"What business is it of mine to judge those outside the Church? Are you not to judge those inside? God will judge those outside. 'Expel the wicked man from among you'"* [1 Corinthians 5:12-13]. Hopefully, it will not come to this, but there is a needful course of action that must take place in regard to *"Them"* and *"Us"* so that *"Them"* will no longer be, not because free expression is banned, but because only faithful expression is allowed. *"Them"* are no longer, because they now have a name. They not only identify their concerns, but also identify themselves with such. We do well to remind ourselves, as highlighted previously, when there was a difference over an issue, even a disappointment in conduct, Paul *"opposed* [Peter] *to his face…"* [Galatians 2:11]. Paul did not write an anonymous letter, nor did he go behind Peter's back, neither did he get someone else to do it. Nowhere in the Bible are we encouraged to solve disputes, disappointments, and differences, anonymously, and certainly not, in the first instance, indirectly:

> *"…if you are offering your gift at the altar and there remember that your*

*brother has something against you, leave your gift there in front of the altar.
First go and be reconciled to your brother; then come and offer your gift. Settle
matters quickly with your adversary....*

*...If your brother sins against you, go and show him his fault, just between
the two of you. If he listens to you, you have won your brother over. But if he will
not listen, take one or two others along, so that 'every matter may be established
by two or three witnesses.' If he refuses to listen to them, tell it to the church;
and if he refuses to listen even to the church, treat him as you would a pagan
or a tax collector."*
[Matthew 5:23-25 & 18:15-17]

The common denominator of what Jesus is saying is that of direct and
personal contact – not only an awareness of the grievance but also of who
the offended and disgruntled party is. How can there ever be reconciliation
in anonymity? At every point, the persons involved are identified, and their
claims verified, and a solution jointly pursued.

It is long since overdue, that our congregations be instructed from the
Scriptures as to what kind of behaviour will be encouraged and that mode
of behaviour which is unacceptable, both being reinforced in practice. In
the short term, it will not be pleasant, and more than just the pastor will be
the target of *"Them"*, in the final twists and turns of that carnal *"machine's"*
death throes – but that such must be stopped in its tracks and stripped of its
platform is a debate and denial we do not have the luxury of any more, as if
we ever did.

Jesus says:
*"This is the verdict: Light has come into the world, but men loved darkness
instead of light because their deeds were evil. Everyone who does what is evil
hates the light, and will not come into the light for fear that his deeds will be
exposed. But whoever lives by the truth comes into the light, so that it may be
seen plainly that what he has done has been done through God."*
[John 3:19-21]

God never works in the *"darkness"* but is always *"overcoming the darkness"* [John 1:5] by calling us out of the *"darkness"* in delivering us from it. The Church has to live in the *"light"*. By the very nature of how they operate, *"Them"* reside in the *"darkness."* To demand that if they want to be heard they must also be seen, invites *"Them"* to come out into the *"light"*. By insisting on the *"light,"* *"dark"* ways are renounced, everyone becomes part of the solution, because *"Them,"* along with *"Us"* have now become *"We!"* and God is glorified.

In The Meantime…!

The chances are that the unmasking discovery of *"Them"* will be to us, and all, the similar anticlimax that the Wizard of Oz was to Dorothy and her three friends – a small, old man, hiding behind a curtain {*"The Wizard Of Oz,"* c.1939, MGM}. *"Them"* are rarely more than just the thrown voices of our equivalent *"Sanballat"* and *"Tobiah"*! This, however, does not diminish the wrong they do nor the torment they cause pastors.

In the meantime – and it often is a *"mean"* time - hold on, weary and *"Broken Pastor"*! In regard to his *"Them"* Nehemiah prayed, *"Now strengthen my hands."* [Nehemiah 6:9] You need to do the same.

Remember, that what is of God never comes in the *"darkness"* – therefore, don't reason with it. In the same way that Western Governments will not negotiate with terrorists, so Pastors and Church Leaders should never negotiate with *"Church Terrorists!"* That's who *"Them"* are - they terrorize, they lurk in the darkness. Pastor, try not to be weary and afraid over *"Them,"* and do not surrender to *"Them,"* especially by abdication through negotiation – *"…what do righteousness and wickedness have in common? Or what fellowship can light have with darkness?"* [2 Corinthians 6:14]. We must recognize these things with all the consequences of what their unmasking means – *"Have nothing to do with the fruitless deeds of darkness, but rather expose them"* [Ephesians 5:11] If God works only in the *"light"*, according to the *"light,"* must not also His *"household"*? [1 Timothy 3:15]

"There's an enemy who seeks to kill what he can't control,
he twists and turns, making mountains out of molehills –
But I will call on the Lord,
Who is worthy of praise,
I run to Him,
And I am saved!"

{"Outrageous Grace," by Godfrey Birtill, c. Godfrey Birtill, Thankyou Music UK}

"Run to Him," pastor, *"run to Him"* – He will *"strengthen your hands."*

Yours in *"the fellowship of His sufferings,"*
The Broken Pastor!

CHAPTER 9
MONDAY MORNING LETTERS

"O LORD, You deceived me, and I was deceived; You overpowered me and prevailed. I am ridiculed all day long; everyone mocks me. Whenever I speak, I cry out proclaiming violence and destruction. So the word of the LORD has brought me insult and reproach all day long."
[Jeremiah 20:7-8]

As pastor-preachers we glean a lot of information from many sources. Despite our best efforts, we are not always able to establish or remember where it all comes from. It is in this regard that many years ago I came across a sole statistic which I have never forgotten even though I cannot recall the origin. The statistic seemed to confirm what most pastors often feel and just instinctively, through personal experience, know – it is claimed that more pastors resign on a Monday than any other day of the week. You didn't really need anyone to tell you that, nor is it paramount on this occasion that the source be cited and the study confirmed – even if I could steer you in that direction – we pastors already knew it!

I wonder if it was a *"Monday Morning"* when Jeremiah recorded those words of self-dread and even realization? What pastor, who has been in the ministry for any meaningful amount of time, seeking to be honest and faithful to the *"call of God"*, has not had that *"Monday Morning"* feeling, where it all just seems wearyingly futile and impossible to go on? And, whether in our minds or in actuality, we place that blank piece of paper on our desk to write out our resignation? And, as in all things, just like with Jeremiah, God gets it all first. He is informed before anyone else. We are often there, if not every Monday, on many Mondays....

Life Is About Lumps!

When we sit down and go through the wounds we have received from painful encounters with those we are trying to help, misunderstood motives in what we are seeking to achieve, the sharpness of betrayal from those we trusted and worked close with, the weariness of seeking to do the right thing with no return or improvement in sight, we discover that, more often than not, what results in the *"Monday Morning Letter"* is not any one-off isolated happening, but rather an accumulation of events, over a period of time, from different directions, for a variety of reasons, many of which are inexplicable, and even unjustifiable. Thoughtless words and actions – but no less danger-ous and damaging in their effect – combined also with a constant stream of criticism from other parties, and just the day-in, day-out realities of the pastorate, including a wage which in *"earthly"* terms of return is neither worth the hassle nor in proper relation to the time and effort spent on the job, all eventually take their toll.

Although there is no *"one"* factor that does it, there is a final one – the proverbial *"last straw"* – and it seems to push us too far and we cross a line, we cannot *"go on"*! On its own, *"Mrs. Parker's"* constant whinging about the length of the sermon and the choice of hymns can be coped with.... On its own *"Mr. Barrett's"* barbed comments can be taken in our stride.... On its own the Church spinster, *"Miss. Murray"* and her always being a *"martyr-to-the-cause"* when there's any work needing to be done, so as to take away from the good she does and spoil the team-effort from everyone else, can be overcome.... On its own, the predictable pedantic correction, shouted out from the congregation during the announcements, or pointed out to the pastor about a misprint in the newsletter can be coped with.... On its own, the brashness of *"Mr. Thompson"* who always has to say something, despite his rarely having something to say, can be brushed off.... On its own, the *"easy come, easy go"* attitude of *"Mr & Mrs. Pew Warmer & Family"* who you never see from one Sunday to the next, never caring because they never have a care, is a reality you have long since accepted you cannot change…. On its own, the loud pianist who *"performs"* more than he *"accompanies"* is seen as better than having no pianist at all, and so is accommodated, even *"humoured"*….

How much of the above live in your congregation? But here is the point: On its own…! On its own…! On its own…! It never is *"on its own"*. As pastors we can never minister in isolation, we cannot choose who we serve, we cannot safely pigeon-hole people and neatly pack them off. Life happens – it does not wait to be called and invited. Humanity – including ourselves - does not come to us in the orderliness of an appointment book, the tidiness of a schedule, and the fairness of a rota! Life is not about nicely prepared segments…Life is about LUMPS – it comes in all shapes and sizes and guises, and even, disguises!

When The Analysis Undermines The Diagnosis!

As pastors, we have a commitment to *"be there"* in the crises of life. When people's hearts are broken, when families fall apart, when a person's world is smashed to pieces because of illness and bereavement, when life just doesn't make sense – it is here that the pastor comes in to his own. I have lost count of the number of times I have gone into a terrible situation of human tragedy, overwhelmed, not knowing what to say and even how to be, and every time, God has given strength and wisdom far beyond myself. What pastor has not called upon God in such times and places and not found Him more than sufficient, to the comfort of those we serve, and the amazement of ourselves?

What derails us is not the difficult tasks, the impossible situations, the rawness of people in their genuine desperation – what destroys pastors, truly knocking us over and keeping us *"down"*, is one dose too much, one encounter too often, with the greatest church and ministry saboteur of all – PETTINESS! Time and again, the acknowledged presence of it fools us – the analysis undermines the diagnosis! *"Oh, it's only 'Mrs…'!"* *"It's just 'Mr…!"* *"That's how she's always been!"* *"That's just his way!"* On its own, it is petty, but allowed to continue, given the freedom to accumulate and combine with other more noteworthy concerns – pastors get seriously damaged and worn down, ministries needlessly wrecked, churches helplessly abandoned.

As a pastor I have often wished I could take some people around with me for just one week and then they would realize that when you are given to see and know and deal with some of what a pastor has to in the reality of life and death and Heaven and hell, then it really doesn't matter what colour the walls of the church hall are, or how the young people dress. Having drums in the services is not the last stand issue many think it is, neither is what version of the Bible is used. The position of the piano and the size of the pulpit, and being afraid to move or change such because it was named after someone or given in *"memory"* are not all that big a deal. And what he didn't get his way over twenty years ago is not as pressing as was thought.

Much of what the church loses sleep over - as well as people, time, effort, and money, not to mention most crucial of all, souls – is of no consequence to Heaven, but will be judged over by Heaven, no less. We not only need to spare ourselves from pettiness but save the people we serve from coming under judgment because of it. We must no longer diminish the analysis of what lies behind our *"Monday Morning Letters"*, because we let it undermine the diagnosis – the cumulative paralysis of pettiness.

The best word on pettiness I have so far come across is from the pen of Mike Yaconelli:

"Petty people are ugly people. They are people who have lost their vision. They are people who have turned their eyes away from what matters and focused, instead, on what doesn't matter. The result is that the rest of us are immobilized by their obsession with the insignificant...."

{"The Wittenburg Door" ed. By Mike Yaconelli, December 1984/January 1985, quoted by Charles Swindoll in "Day By Day with Charles Swindoll," c. 2000, Word Publishing, p.294}

How true this is – the pathetic irony of being around and influenced by petty people is that we become paralysed and ensnared by the intensity of their *"smallness"*, having life and positivity – even the will to live - stolen from us in seeking to pacify and enlighten them. How long will it take us to learn?: DIFFICULT PROBLEMS CAN OFTEN BE SOLVED – DIFFICULT PEOPLE CAN NEVER BE SATISFIED! Yaconelli continues:

"…Pettiness has become a serious disease in the Church of Jesus Christ – a disease which continues to result in terminal cases of discord, disruption, and destruction. Petty people are dangerous people because they appear to be only a nuisance instead of what they really are – a health hazard."

Pastor, Before You Write That Letter, Consider….

•   You are in good company – not only do you stand shoulder to shoulder with God's faithful servant, Jeremiah, but you stand by the side of God's beloved Son, Jesus Christ. He too knew the weariness of the way, about the slowness of disciples, and the carnal pettiness of people – *"O unbelieving generation, how long shall I stay with you? How long shall I put up with you?..."* [Mark 9:19] We know that oftentimes Jesus took Himself away for private prayer – how much of that felt need in Jesus was to do with the seriously damaging pettiness of carnal humanity, which, in the light of what He had come to do, was a dangerous nonsense, being so hard to bear with, and go on in-spite of? Perhaps, for us too, some respite in the face of this lurking parasite that would otherwise suck the life out of us, if not also the only response to it, is found in identifying and following the same felt need as Jesus habitually pursued.

•   *"What else could I do anyway?"* – how often have we pastors had to own up to this one? Of course, there are other jobs we could do, but not with the same passion, giving the same fulfilment. Life would become very dull and flat, fatally non-stretching and tediously undemanding. When we are in the thick of it we long for such, but that is where, for us, true futility resides. Being a pastor is not only what we have been called to and trained in, but also born for…just like Jeremiah – *"Before I formed you in the womb I knew you, before you were born I set you apart; I appointed you…"* [Jeremiah 1:5]. If we don't believe that, then the best thing, for all, we can do is to get out as soon as possible!

•   *"Still the best job in the world!"* – read that phrase again. It is not posed as a question or suggestion, but stated as a conviction of fact. To know the hand of God upon you. To experience the inspiration of the Holy Spirit.

To live with the anointing of God, in seeing a miracle every day, even if it's just the miracle of what you know God enables you to do. To be charged with the responsibility of opening and declaring the words of God from His Book! To be given trusted access into the carefully guarded, because they are precious, places of people's lives, seeing them at their worst and their best. To help lead a soul to God. To help others grow in grace. To bear witness to the vows of a husband and wife. To dedicate to God the new life of a baby. To commend to God the soul of a departed loved one. To have a part in a work that truly will last forever. No humanly ordained appointment can give you this, nor can any other pay packet, no matter its greater size, make up for this lack or even loss.

What we must always seek to remember, because we must come to ultimately understand it, is that our reaching for the *"Monday Morning Letter"* does not diminish or deny the genuineness of our call to service and continuance in ministry – it affirms it. To want to write the "Monday Morning Letter" on any day is never the final and truthful word on us and our faithfulness, but what we do with it will be. To put it back in the drawer – even for another time – but going on today, no matter what we are facing, despite how we may or may not be feeling, is what it means to be called of God and kept by God as we remain for God in faithfulness, trust, humility, and even necessity. We too must surely find it, as Jeremiah did, when he laid aside his *"Monday Morning Letter"* because of the Divine necessity that had so marked out his life – *"But if I say, 'I will not mention Him or speak any more in His Name,' His word is in my heart like a fire, a fire shut up in my bones. I am weary of holding it in; indeed, I cannot"* [Jeremiah 20:9]. Here, for us, is the dynamic compulsion we cannot live without through walking away from, but have to return and submit ourselves to, over and over again…even beginning every Monday!

The classic words of Jordan Grooms are timeless in their validity:
"When God calls you to be a missionary, don't stoop to be a king!"

Yours in *"the fellowship of His sufferings,"*
The Broken Pastor!

CHAPTER 10

MANSE MATTERS

"By wisdom a house is built, and through understanding it is established;
through knowledge its rooms are filled with rare and beautiful treasures."
[Proverbs 24:3-4]

I have always been thankful for the Christian home in which I grew up and this wonderful heritage is one that, by the grace of God, has continued into my own adult life as a spouse and parent. There are many who have not had the same blessed nurture of a godly environment throughout their entire lives. They have come in to it through the later conversion of their parents or themselves. But for me it was already established. I was born into it. I am very grateful for the atmosphere of genuine godliness I have always been a part of and surrounded by at home, even now, being a product of.

Some years ago there was a pastor in Aberdeen, Scotland who was having a rough time, to say the least. He had taken an unpopular, but right, stance on a vital moral issue. Very soon it caught the attention of the media, who relentlessly pursued this minister in a very unfair and harsh manner. Sadly this has become the norm for us today. He was under great pressure. One day a friend asked him how he was getting on. His friend enquired, *"How do you cope with all this negative publicity?"* The minister quietly replied, *"Because things are so good at home!"*

How true that needs to be, in every walk of life, but none more so than the pastor with his family. *"Manse Matters"* – it really does! The manse has been described as *"living in a goldfish bowl"* where everybody sees and knows and seems to have a say – from the amount you are paid, to how much is spent on the fabric of the house, not to mention the colour and style of the interior. Pathetically, there are always those who are on hand to remind the pastor and his family that *"the manse does not belong to them,"* it is *"not their home!"* The manse has also been likened to *"living above the shop"* where you never seem to get away from the job – and pastors with their families do need to have a time and space where they can get away even if they do not go away. There have been times in the life of this pastor when the manse has felt like a ball and chain. When the Apostle Paul was in prison he was chained to a Roman guard. In the same way, pastors, in regard to manses, can often feel manacled – if they give up the job they are out of a home. And those bonds are never tighter than when there are those in the manse who would leave if they could, but have no place to go.

At this point, may I address a pressing issue that pastors and congregations together need to deal with sooner as opposed to later? We pastors know that *"we are not in it for the money!"* Whilst we appreciate the salaries we do receive, understanding the faithful and sacrificial giving of many to make that possible, we do accept that we are not going to be paid on a par with other professionals with their degrees. This also means that any pension plan a Church or denomination may have in place, whilst again being welcomed, is not, when the time comes, going to be enough to live on never mind help buy a property to live in. For any person, never mind a pastor, to start taking on the burden of a mortgage in his early sixties is so unfair and not right. It is, nevertheless, the depressing reality for many ageing pastors.

In these last years, pastors have been wisely encouraged to look at investing in some kind of property of their own, so they will have some secure investment for the future that is more than financial, but literally, concrete! This could also be instead of living in a traditional church manse, where the church as long as the pastor is in their employment, in place of the running costs of owning a manse and paying for its upkeep themselves, help pay a portion of the pastor's mortgage in a *"like for like"* arrangement (such would obviously have to be in accordance with the relevant tax regulations). For even though it is the pastor who will own the house, it will, to all intents and purposes, be used as a manse. This arrangement, apart from giving the pastoral family a much needed foot on the property ladder, also gives them the space, freedom, and privacy of a place that is their *"own."* It also means that when he is no longer pastoring that local church, his family still have a home. This becomes very important with children and maintaining the stability of their education, potentially avoiding the needless upheaval of changing schools at what could be a vital stage of learning for them.

Another arrangement that has worked well for some is a *"part-owner-ship"* of the manse where, for example, the church may own sixty percent and the pastor forty percent. Whilst reducing the financial burden on both parties, this does have the potential for thorny problems in the future when the church and pastor part company, particularly if it is acrimonious.

It is difficult enough with the already low stipends of pastors and diminishing incomes of many Churches, through Tithes and Offerings, to deal with these matters. But as good stewards, we have to face up to them honestly and responsibly, while options remain and there is time. Congregations would do well to consider: does a Church only have a caring responsibility for a pastor and his family for as long as they are actively and locally serving them? We rightly talk about the on-going general responsibility of care pastors should always have for the church, but what about the continuing responsibility of care from churches for their pastors, especially retired pastors, who have given their whole lives to service, in many cases, foregoing the wages and thus standards of living that would have been considerably higher had they served the *"world"* with their gifts and abilities? Perhaps it would be a good exercise for both pastors and churches to seriously look at and take on board the merits afforded by the Scriptures recording of a Shunammite wife who said to her husband in regard to God's prophet Elisha: *"I know that this man who often comes our way is a holy man of God. Let's make a small room on the roof and put in it a bed and a table, a chair and a lamp for him. Then he can come and stay there whenever he comes to us"* [2 Kings 4:9-10]. Here is a "*selah*" moment for the whole church – pastors and people – to "*consider these things.*"

Keeping It In The Family!

Like it or not, "*called*" or not, pastoral ministry is a family affair, affecting and demanding something from every member of the family. Like with most other matters of life, it is not unless or until you actually live in the manse that you come to realize how much the manse, and the lives within it, matter. How many have considered the prospects for the pastor's wife, who has committed herself to a lifetime of listening to the same preacher and having the same pastor? She can neither move Churches or call for a new pastor! How many have recognized the conflicting issues of children growing into young people? That's hard enough for any child, but when your dad is also your pastor…?

For this pastor, like with many, the real "*hero*" of the manse is in fact a "*heroine*" - the pastor's wife – often, certainly in public gatherings, having to look after and train the children on her own. It's one thing to suffer and be "*broken*", but there is a very real sense in which it is harder and costlier and even more painful to have to look on at close quarters as the love of your life goes through it, not being able to do anything about it to stop it, but to have to stand there and support, and often in silence as far as any public utterance is concerned. I remember when I was preparing to graduate from Bible College and I went for an interview with one of the Superintendents of the denomination I served to talk through some possible placement options for my first pastorate. I was engaged at the time, soon to be married. My Superintendent said to me, "*Whatever you do, wherever you go, make sure your wife is happy with the manse. This is her special domain. If things are right there, many obstacles will be overcome, problems solved, battles settled, and victories won!*" He was right. We male pastors – and that is the only perspective from which I can write on this – need to be aware of the needs of our wives to be a woman and to make a home, even if it is in a manse. The church too needs to recognize this and not make the pastor's wife out to be "unreasonable" in her requests and expectations.

The great heritage of the manse belongs to the children. I have met many pastor's children who, because of what they witnessed and were deprived of when growing up in the manse, are now deeply hurting and terribly twisted in bitterness towards the church and resentment towards God at what was *"allowed"* to happen. As a pastor with children who have yet to leave home, there has been much we have to protect them from. However, growing up in the manse has taught them the precious life values of kindness, consideration, integrity, and sacrifice. We need to equip our children – whether they live in a manse or not – with the right tools that they may live well. Our children need to know that this world does not owe them anything, but that, as God's children – pastor's children or not – we have an obligation to show Christ to the world. Living in a manse has given, by learned experience, our children the knowledge of the need to share what we have with those who don't have. One of my regrets is that I have not always got the balance right in these matters. There are, sadly, those who are pastoral *"parasites"* – if they are not always calling you out, they are always seeking to come in. They will take you for everything you've got – from family time, to even almost moving in with the family, as part of the family, if they ever got their way. Only the wisdom that is from God will ever get the balance right. There are needs at home which need guarding that our children will not be detrimentally spoiled. We should not feel guilty nor allow the unenlightened demands of others to make us feel guilty, when once in a while, we make a choice over them and for our families. The reaffirming message this sends, not only to those in the home, but to others outside about the *"Home"* and *"Family"*, is one of the most vital we will ever communicate, and there is none better we can be committed to. At the end of the day, the church will always get another pastor – my children will not get another dad!

I believe with all my heart that my children do not need to leave the manse as *"damaged goods"* because of what they have experienced and witnessed living there. On the human level, the greater part of that is down to me and the discipline of how I will use my time, the wisdom of my clear priorities, and the security of my own standing and calling in Christ to risk disappointing others when it is wisest to say *"No!"* to them. I must be faithful to the promise I made in my marriage vows before God and in the dedication of my children to God in staying committed to the sacred task of validating, nurturing, and protecting those who have a greater need of me than any congregation I will ever pastor. I do not want the legacy for my children to be that of a pastor who was so busy running after everybody else's children to *"save"* them to the neglect and loss of his own. Scripturally and historically, the home predates the church. There is no real distinction because there is no genuine conflict - such are only *"imagined"* and imposed because we are not wise. As households of faith, if we cannot be the Church at home with all which must be embraced there, then we are not the Church any place else, no matter who and what is being taken up there.

Keeping The Family In It!

There will be times, when individually, or as a complete unit, every one in the family will want to get out! When the children of the manse grow in to the young people of the manse, and there are things which, as parents, we can no longer hide from them, and they see how some treat their dad and hear some of the comments made, even by other young people in the church who just repeat what they hear their own parents saying, is it any wonder that they want out? The constant need for tight budgeting can also be wearing. It would be nice, every once in a while for many pastors and their wives if they could just spontaneously and joyfully treat their children to a 'MacDonald's' or something as basic as that, without having to weigh up what other thing will have to be forfeited because, yes, money is that tight! Outside the manse, most just have no idea because these *"simple joys"* are not matters which directly concern them with theirs, and are taken lightly, even thoughtlessly in regard to others.

Rob Parsons and the ministry organization Care For The Family are incredible. The families God has rescued through their ministry only Heaven will reveal. Rob Parson's books are a *"must"* for all pastors. In his book *"What They Didn't Teach Me In Sunday School,"* Parsons shares a painful encounter he had, an experience many will automatically relate to. A lady approached him and suggested how *"ironic"* it would be if, after all he and his wife have sought to do in promoting and protecting the welfare of the *"family"*, their own children went astray. Parsons writes:

"... I thought I detected in her voice a slight hope that they would. The truth is, it wouldn't be ironic at all.... Many church leaders face this. Their children are not allowed to be like other people's children. Because they are the leader's children the congregation demand they behave five levels above normal – and it's wrong." {"What They Didn't Teach Me In Sunday School," by Rob Parsons, c. 1997, 2000. Published by Hodder & Stoughton, p.127}.

There is one pastor reading this who really needs to heed these words from Parsons. God save us all from being enslaved to maintaining an outward image – which is not real – at the expense of forsaking being right at home and real for those who live there.

Of course, our children need boundaries and standards. But they also need the freedom to push up against them, and test them, proving their meaning and worth for themselves. Our children need the allowance of failure and the true learning that comes, often by the reality of their mistakes. Without diminishing sin, how many have wrongly rushed to a damningly unfair conclusion about their children, when what they were expressing and going through was a phase, which, if not written off as they were, they would soon have given up and returned 'home' from, but who have been so chastised and ostracised to have nothing to come back to? God help us.

"They felt good eyes upon them
And shrank within – undone;
'Good parents had good children,'
And they – a wandering one.

The good folks never meant
To act smug or condemn,
But having prodigals
Just 'wasn't done' with them.

Remind them gently, Lord,
How You have trouble with Your children too."
{By Ruth Graham Bell, quoted in "Fresh Elastic For Stretched Out Mums,"
by Barbara Johnson, c.1986. Published by Marshall Pickering, pp. 98-99}

Likewise, how little it is reckoned of the great assault from hell set against Christian marriages in general and of pastors in particular. When a pastoral marriage fails, the fall-out effects, domestically and congregationally, are much greater in their destructive impact. At the time of writing, within days of each other, this pastor is aware of another two break-ups in the marriages of pastors and church leaders.

Whilst we all understand the ultimate need to take personal responsibility for our actions, there is a responsibility of awareness and prayer-filled protection which the congregation needs to seriously take on as champions and protectors of the pastoral family. The questions needing to be asked and acted upon by congregations are like the following:

• Are we covering our pastor and spouse with intelligent prayer, asking God to protect their marriage, keeping it alive in love, faithfulness, passion, beauty, and joy?
• Are we praying for the pastor's children, that we will never be a stumbling block to them, that God will deliver them from all evil?
• Are we praying for angelic protection for the manse, recognizing that this is a family satan is sure to hate and out to destroy?
• Are we practically, fairly, and faithfully recognizing the needs of our pastoral family – the needs of the wife to make a home, and the needs of the children to have a home and to be children, the right of a pastor and his family to privacy, stability, and a duty to be cared for?
• Are we willing to let the pastor and his family live in an accommodation that is of a lower standard than we ourselves would ever be willing to live in?
• Do we extend to the pastor and his what is right or only what is left?
• When we close the door to our homes, enjoying all we do and have

worked for, do we consider what the pastor is living in behind the closed door of the manse, which he might have otherwise had as his "own" had he chosen to work for the benefit of himself and not for the blessing of us?

The fact is – *"Manse Matters!"*
The matters of the manse do not rest so much on RIGHTS as they do on REASONS….

Yours in *"the fellowship of His sufferings,"*
The Broken Pastor!

EPILOGUE
THROUGH IT ALL...!

"...becoming like Him in His death...."
[Philippians 3:10]

The Apostle Paul's one striking phrase captures the reality of what it means to be *"broken"*; the reason why pastors get *"broken"*; and the result of our *"brokenness"* in where it can lead - that we may *"...know Christ...becoming like Him in His death...."*

"Broken Pastor," Hold On....You'll Be So Glad You Did!

The essence of all I have been trying to write has not come as result of referring to books on a shelf but from listening to the story of my heart, allowing it to honestly speak. Most pastors, including me, have problems with personal honesty – not in regard to the integrity of our characters but in giving ourselves permission to hurt and to need and to show and share our scars, our fears and tears, as well as our triumphs and trophies. We pastors, who are charged with communicating truth are often less forthcoming in the truth about ourselves, and especially between ourselves. We are undermined and undone by our own needless sense of insecurity, especially with each other.

We encourage those who hear us preach to become *"vulnerable"* and to *"open up," "seek help,"* and *"be accountable,"* while many of us have barricaded and hidden ourselves and our needs behind our *"lofty positions"*, being a slave to the delusion that not only can the pastor not have any close friends but that he must also never show weakness, always know what to do, having it all together and in place, never missing a beat. Whilst some of the reasons we do this are to do with the subtlety of undetected pride, that if we talk frankly we will disappoint people and our honest admissions will ultimately come back to bite us, destroying our ambitions and prospects for advancement – what the world calls *"promotion"* – there are other factors involved. We are so often backward in the coming forward with ourselves because we genuinely do not want to make it about self, we don't want to get in the way. We have to recognize that it was not only Jesus Who was *"incarnate"*. There is a very real sense in which the whole Gospel is *"incarnational"* – being displayed in the flesh and blood, gutsy truth of genuinely living where others live, as the down to earth and *"ordinary"*, real people we are. The people we preach to and pastor have money worries too, they get tired and *"broken"*, they have fears, they are misunderstood, they live in the midst of perplexing contradiction, with issues which remain painfully unresolved, they have trouble with the children, and stress points in their marriages. Perhaps the unrealistic expectations which many pastors crumble under would be corrected if more pastors would confront them instead of impossibly trying to conform to them, because neither they nor the expectations are real!

Pastor, it is okay to be *"broken"*! It's alright not always to have the answers, whether it be for others or about yourself. It is not a sin to want to give up and walk away. It is not to dishonour God and be unfaithful to your parishioners if you get weary and fed up. It is not down to a spiritual *"lack"* that satan assaults you at every turn. Neither the sky will fall in nor do your congregation come apart if you show to them the *"down"* side, the difficult side, even the *"dark"* side of your humanity and the struggle of it, once in a while. None of the above are a reason for bailing out, but are the testimony, even the promise, of why you must keep going and hold on – you will be so glad you did!

Most of us, and more than once, will have preached from that mighty 11th Chapter of Hebrews – *"The Gallery Of The Faithful!"* What a record of overcoming faith. However, we often miss and thus forget, that there is also a place in here for the *"broken"* ones. In the midst of verse 35 of Hebrews 11, there is a change of reference and pace:

"...OTHERS were tortured and refused to be released....Some faced jeers and flogging, while still others were chained and put in prison. They were stoned; they were sawed in two; they were put to death by the sword. They went about...destitute, persecuted and mistreated....They wandered....These were all commended for their faith, yet none of them received what had been promised. God had planned something better for us so that only together with us would they be made perfect."

[Hebrews 11:35-40]

Not only do we frequently skim over this, but we also stop short at the end of Chapter 11, not recognizing that the application continues in to Hebrews 12:

"Therefore, since we are surrounded by such a great cloud of witnesses [those mentioned in Hebrews 11], *let us throw off everything that hinders and the sin that so easily entangles, and let us run with perseverance the race marked out for us. Let us fix our eyes on Jesus, the author and perfecter of our faith* [and also the Supreme Witness of the Faithful], *Who for the joy set before Him endured the cross* [being *"broken"*], *scorning its shame, and sat down at the right hand of God. Consider Him Who endured such opposition from sinful men, so that you will not grow weary and lose heart."*

[Hebrews 12:1-3]

What are *"the great cloud of witnesses,"* including Jesus, saying to us who are now walking and living and enduring where they did?: *"KEEP GOING!... DON'T GIVE UP!...HOLD ON!...YOU'LL BE SO GLAD YOU DID!...IT IS WORTH IT!"*

"When I Get Older...!"

Have we ever stopped to consider the possibility that most of the anger we encounter from other people and experience in ourselves, has more to do with the hurt of brokenness than anything else?

Being *"broken"* will either make us bitter or better! If we go through life and ministry clinging to the rights of self the process of breaking, we all go through, will only cause us to be bitter. On the other hand, if we surrender ourselves and cling to the Reason, Who is Jesus, the brokenness we endure will make us better. The Bible says: *"...'God opposes the proud but gives grace to the humble.' Humble yourselves, therefore, under God's mighty hand, that He may lift you up in due time. Cast all your anxiety on Him because He cares for you"* [1 Peter 5:5-7]. We all not only have the potential for that, but also the capacity to miss it.

One of the churches I pastored had just short of ten pastors in the congregation. Some were retired pastors, even some former pastors of that local congregation, whilst others were *"unassigned"*, not being in active service. The ones who should have been the present pastor's most powerful comrades and greatest encouragers became his biggest obstacles, as some allowed themselves to be used as rallying points of discontentment. The blows I suffered from them were second to none. Perhaps the retired pastors just could not let go, or some of the others, having no assignment, thought they could do the job better than I. Perhaps they could, but the reality was, for that time, in that place, they were not the pastor. I was.

If God allows me to live for long enough, the time will come when, in a local church, I will be sitting, as a pastor under the ministry of another pastor, where those pastors once sat with me. To put it bluntly, no matter their reasons or concerns, I don't want to become for anyone else what they became for me. I have said to my wife, on more than one occasion: *"If God spares me and I get old enough to sit in a local church under the ministry of another pastor, and I become a problem for him and a recruiting sergeant for church murmurers, then please put a pillow over my head or put me in a nursing home – at all costs, don't let me continue going to that church!"*

Two highly esteemed elder statesmen of the Church paused to pray with each other after sharing the preaching in a Bible conference. One of them prayed in profound and humble honesty: *"O God, don't let me become a wicked old man!"* {from "Simple Faith," by Charles Swindoll, c.1991. published by Word Books, p.154}. I don't want that to ever become me, but I realize it could. I must not cling to self, but surrender self to Christ!

The Never-Ending Story!

Years ago, Andrae Crouch penned these powerful lyrics:

"I've had many tears and sorrows,
I've had questions for tomorrow,
There have been times I didn't know right from wrong.
But in every situation
God gave blessed consolation
That my trials come to only make me strong.

I've been to lots of places
And I've seen a lot of faces,
There have been times I felt so all alone.
But in those lonely hours,
Yes, those precious lonely hours,
Jesus let me know that I was His own.

So, I thank God for the mountains
And I thank Him for the valleys,
And I thank Him for the storms He's brought me through.
For if I'd never had a problem
I wouldn't know that He could solve them,
I'd never know what faith in God could do.

Through it all,
Through it all
I've learned to trust in Jesus,
I've learned to trust in God.
Through it all,
Through it all
I've learned to depend upon His Word."

{"Through It All," by Andrae Crouch, c.1971, Manna Music Inc.}

This is the Never-Ending Story of our brokenness. As long as there are pastors there will always be *"broken"* ones – it's the world we live in, the people we serve, even the ministry we are called to as we follow the *"example"* Christ left us: *"To this you were called, because Christ suffered for you, leaving you an example, that you should follow in His steps"* [1 Peter 2:21].

Like you, my personal never-ending story is still being written. This book does not conclude it or explain it so much as it expresses it. I am not an *"expert"* in these matters and neither have I *"arrived"*. I am still living with brokenness, even adding to my bruises every day...and I need companions like you along my way. *"Broken Pastor,"* we need to stay at our posts, not only for the honour of our Master – although He is worthy of that alone – and not only for the benefit of those we seek to serve, but also to help one another: *"The Broken Pastors!"*

We live in a world where *"broken"* things are not so much fixed as rubbished and discarded, no longer regarded as being useful. However, in the grace-filled economy of the Kingdom of God, *"The Broken Pastor"* still works!

"I want to know Christ and the power of His resurrection and the fellowship of sharing in His sufferings, becoming like Him in His death, and so, somehow, to attain to the resurrection from the dead. Not that I have already obtained all this, or have already been made perfect, but I press on to take hold of that for which Christ Jesus took hold of me. Brothers, I do not consider myself yet to have taken hold of it. But one thing I do: Forgetting what is behind and straining toward what is ahead, I press on toward the goal to win the prize for which God has called me heavenward in Christ Jesus."
[Philippians 3:10-14]

** All Scripture quotations are from the New International Version, unless otherwise sated **